🦄 ✨Step into a realm where imagination knows no bounds and magic reigns supreme! 🌟✨

Welcome to our mystical creature coloring book, where the extraordinary meets the page, and every stroke holds the promise of enchantment.

🦄 From majestic unicorns to wise and ancient phoenixes, this coloring book is a gateway to a world filled with mythical wonders. Let your creativity take flight as you adorn these magnificent creatures with your own unique touch.

🌟 Whether you're seeking solace in the tranquility of coloring or craving a burst of inspiration, these pages offer an escape to a realm where dreams come to life and the ordinary fades away.

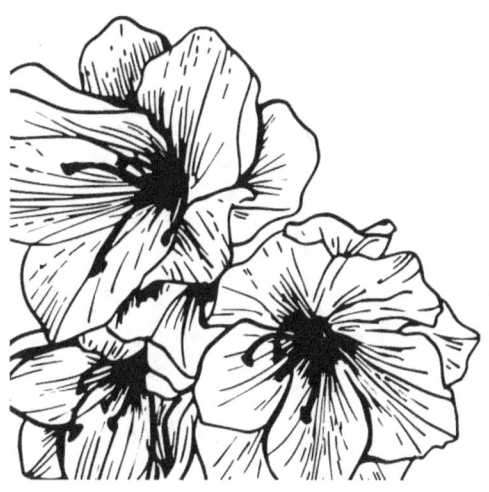

Dive into a kaleidoscope of colors and let your imagination run wild. With each stroke of your pencil or brush, you breathe life into these mystical beings, making them dance with the hues of your choosing.

So, grab your coloring tools and prepare to embark on a journey beyond the confines of reality. Let the magic of this coloring book transport you to a world where anything is possible and the fantastical awaits at every turn of the page.

Are you ready to unlock the door to a world of wonder? The adventure begins now, as you immerse yourself in the enchanting realm of mystical creatures!

Happy coloring!

Dragons

Habitat: Dragons are said to inhabit a variety of environments in folklore, from misty mountains to deep caves and dense forests. Their habitats are often remote and secluded, providing them with ample space to roam and hunt without interference from humans or other creatures.

Food: Dragons are typically portrayed as carnivores, preying on livestock, wild animals, and even humans in some legends. They have voracious appetites and are capable of consuming large quantities of meat in a single meal. Some stories also describe dragons as hoarding treasure, which they guard fiercely and may occasionally consume as a form of sustenance.

Quirky Behaviour: One quirky behaviour commonly associated with dragons is their fondness for shiny objects and precious metals. In many stories, dragons are depicted as hoarders of gold, jewels, and other treasures, which they amass in their lairs. This behaviour is often attributed to their inherent greed and desire for wealth and power. Additionally, dragons are sometimes depicted as having a sense of pride and vanity, particularly when it comes to their appearance and prowess in combat

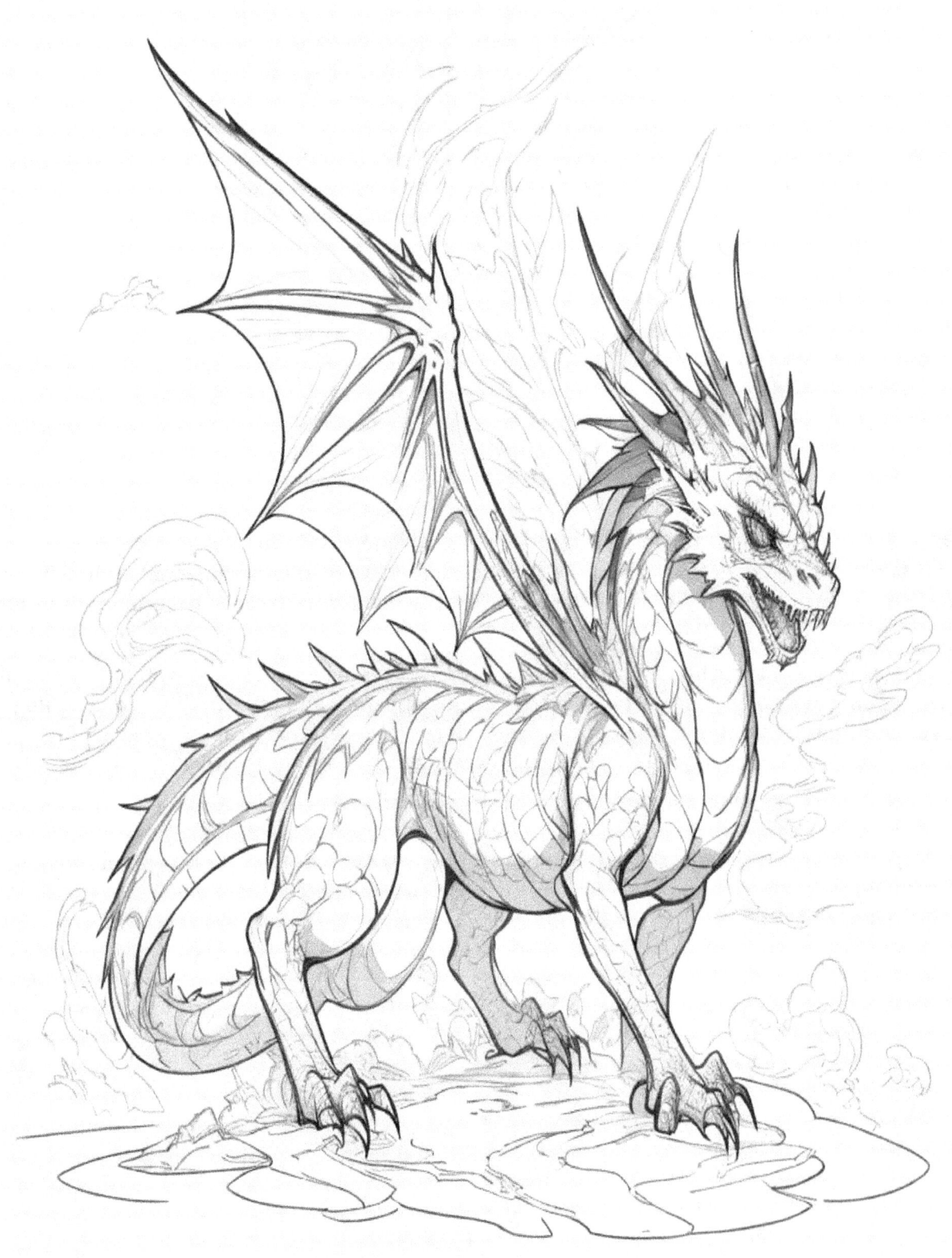

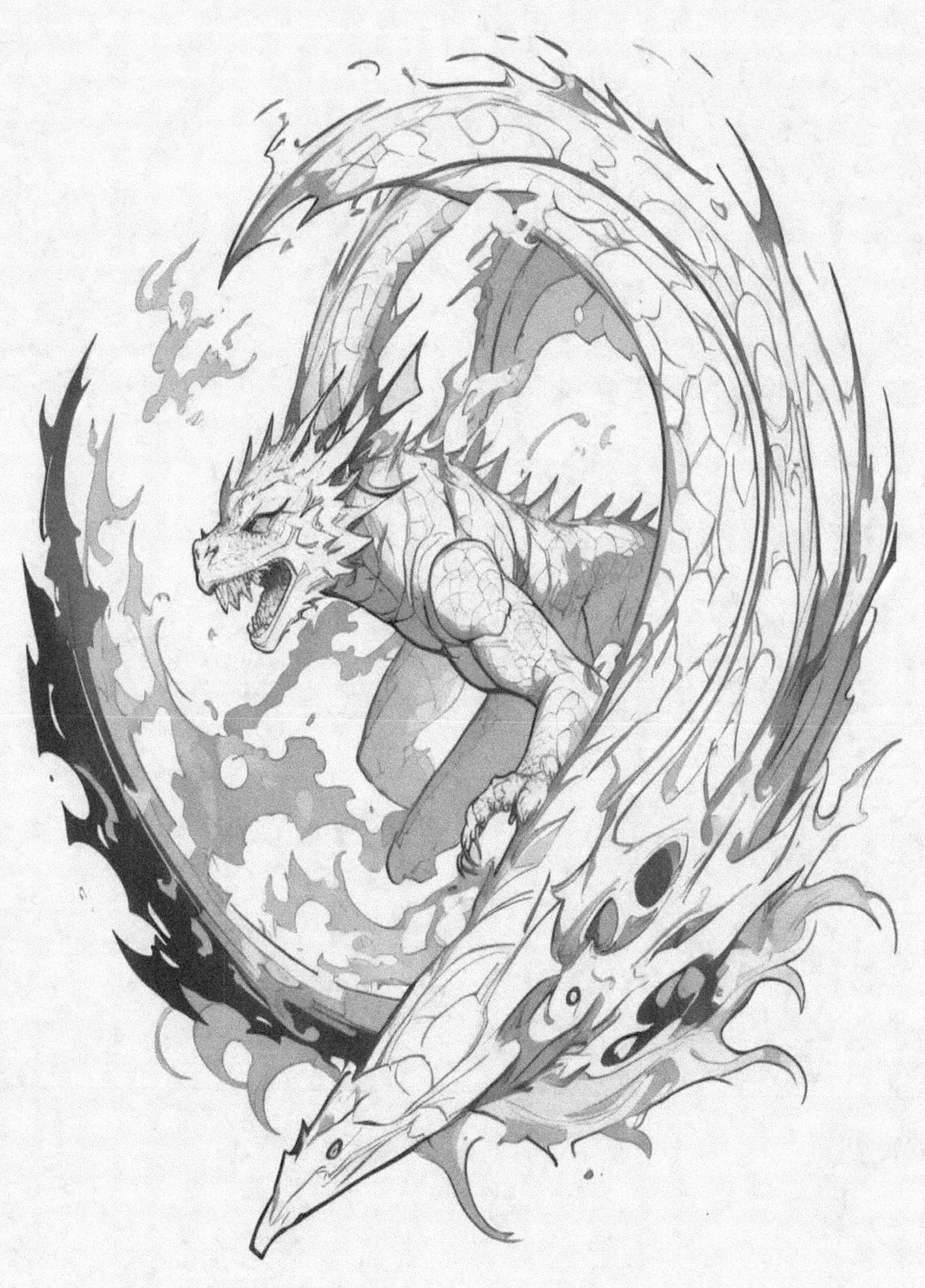

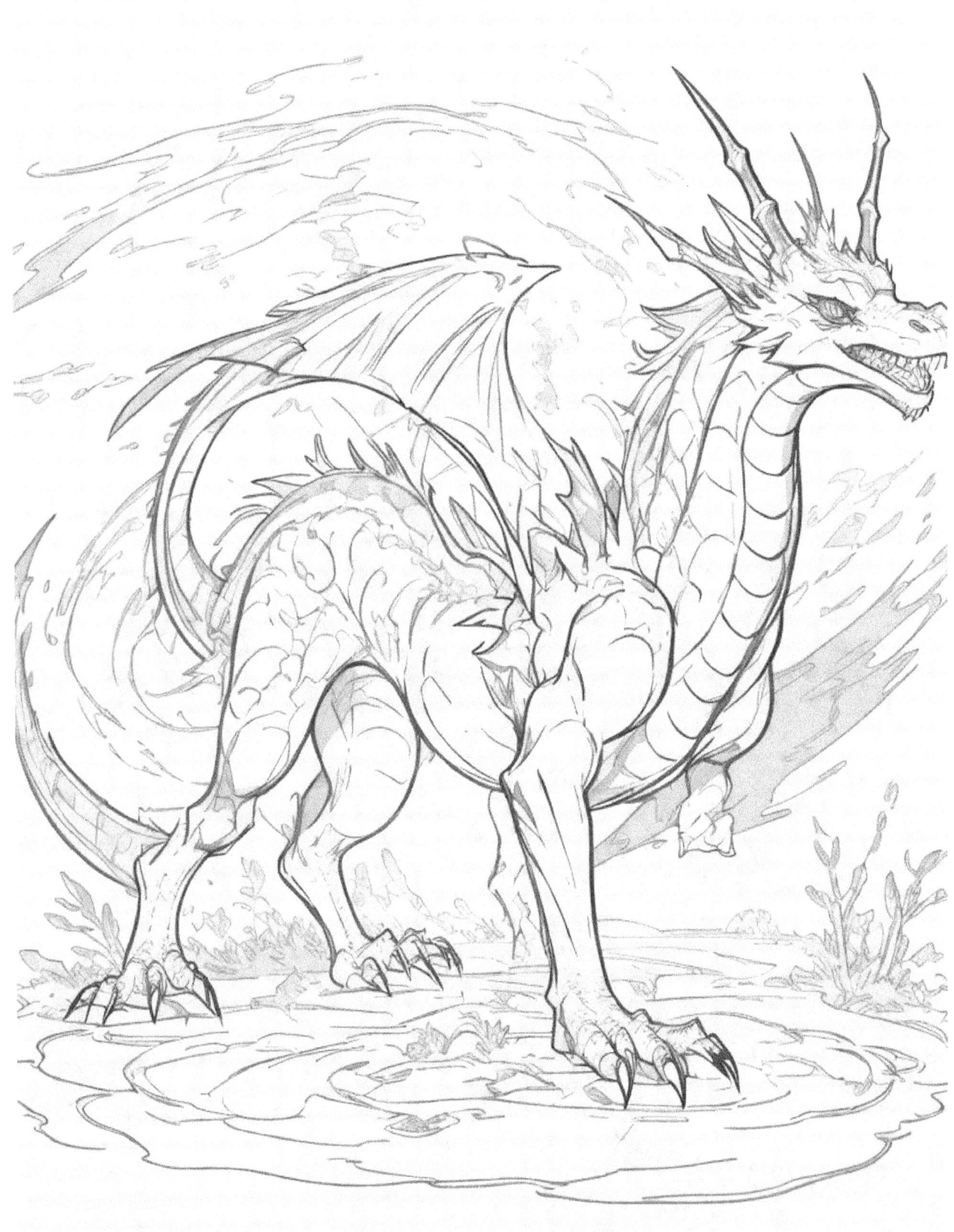

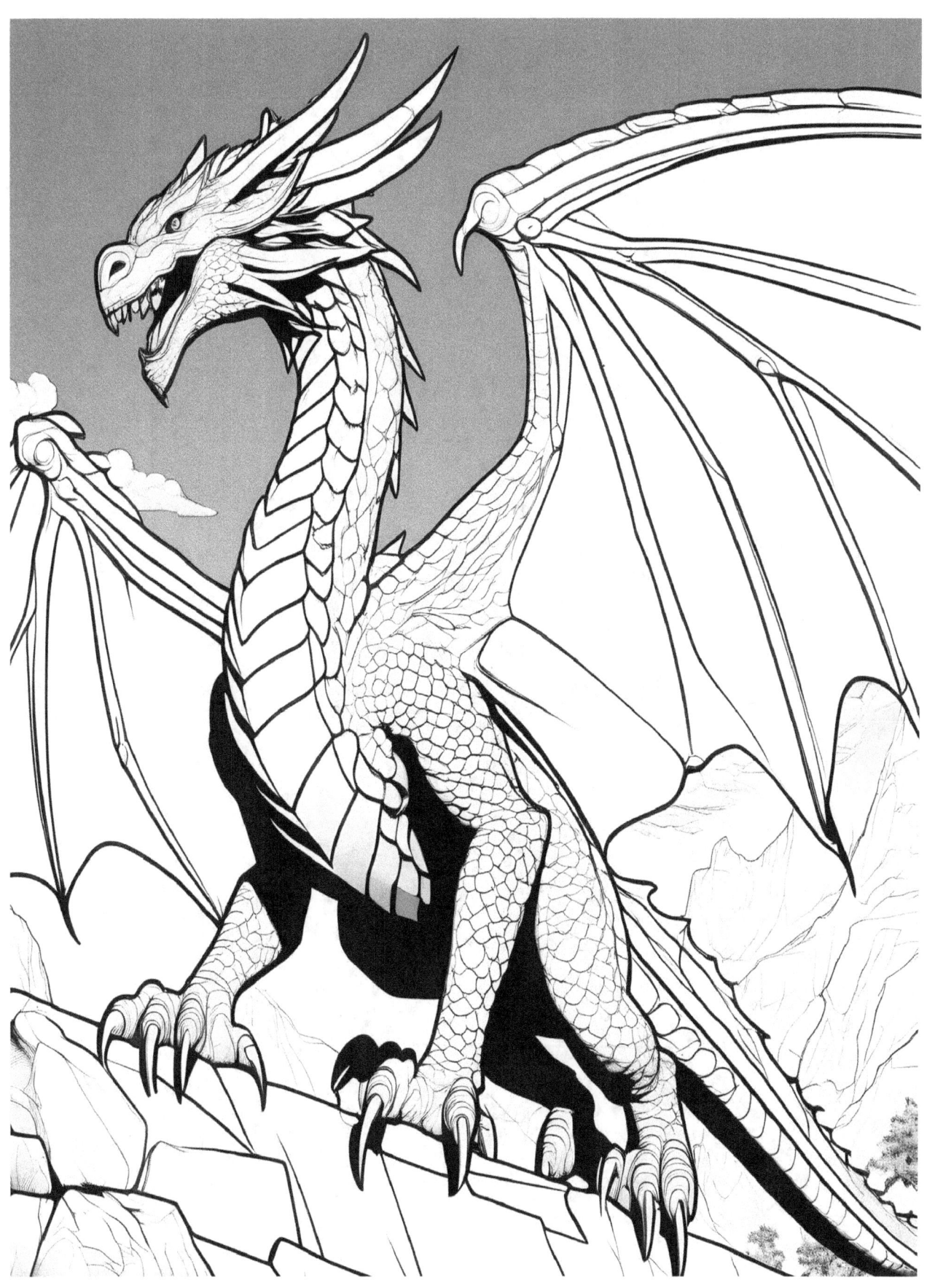

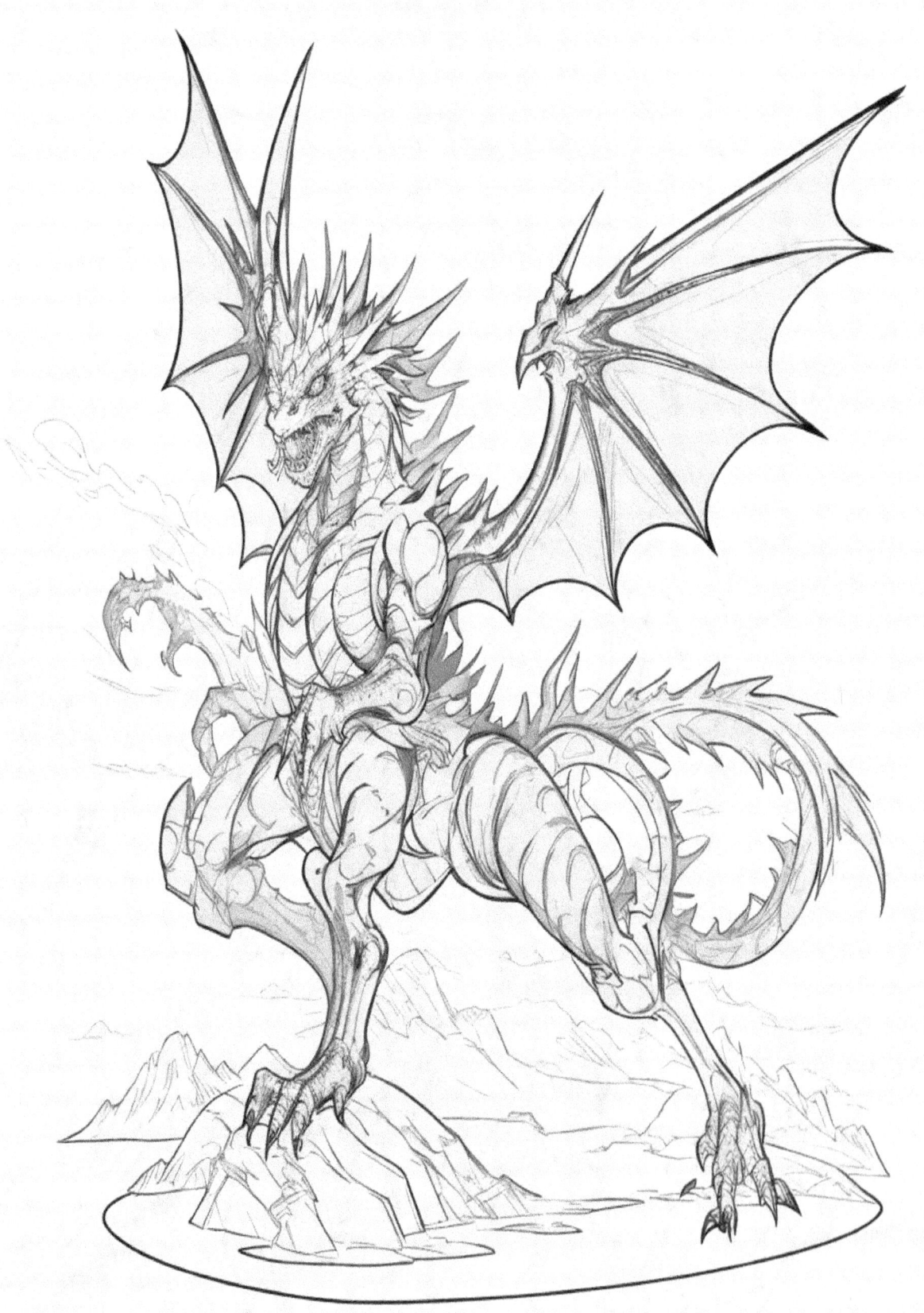

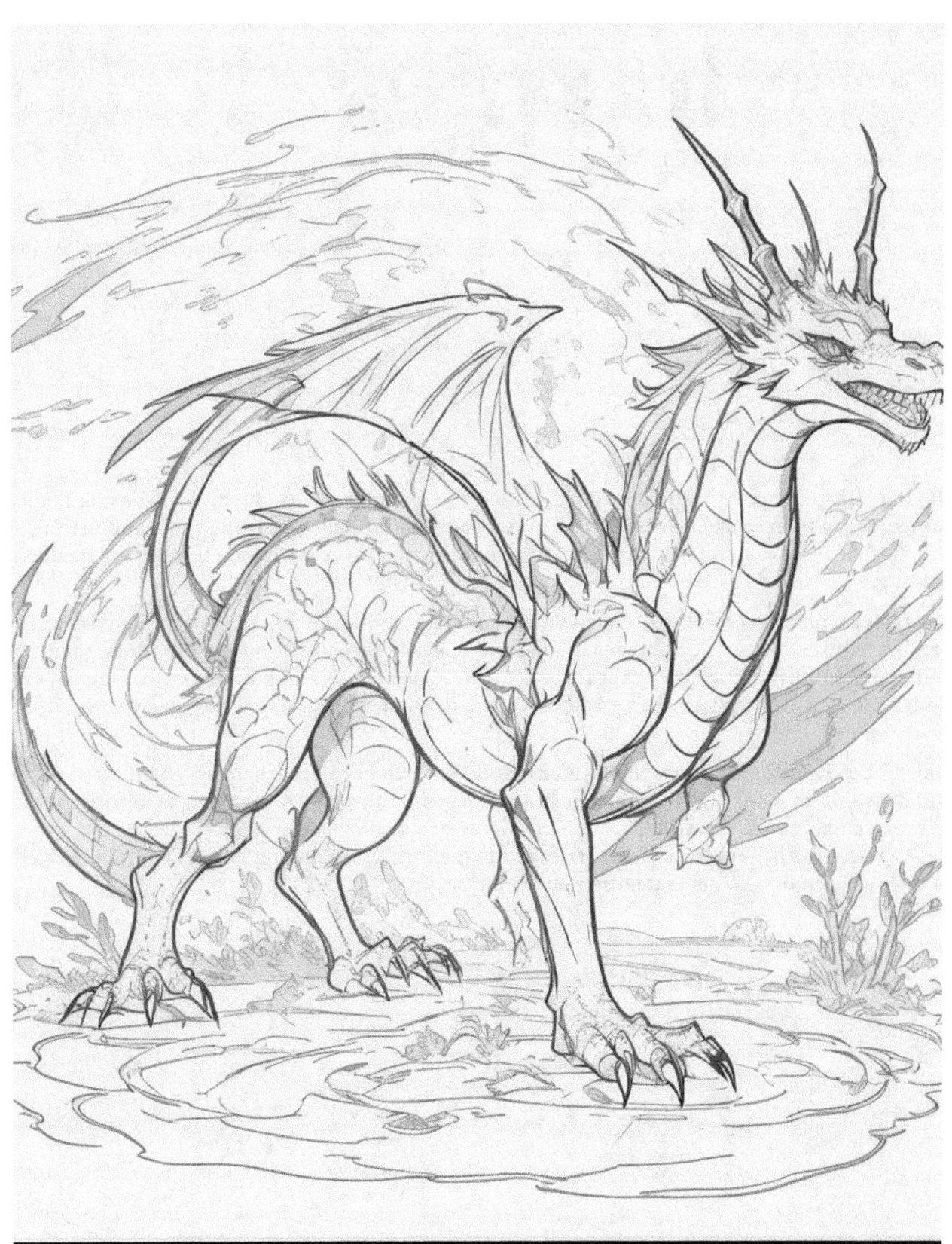

harpies

Habitat: Harpies are typically associated with rugged, remote environments such as mountain ranges, dense forests, and coastal cliffs. These habitats offer ample roosting spots and nesting sites for harpies, who prefer to dwell in areas that provide cover and opportunities for stealthy hunting.

Food: As carnivorous creatures, harpies are known for hunting small animals and occasionally preying on livestock or even humans in folklore. Their diet primarily consists of birds, small mammals, and fish, which they capture using their sharp talons and keen eyesight. Harpies are skilled hunters, capable of swiftly swooping down from the sky to snatch their prey with precision and agility.

Quirky Behaviour: One quirky behaviour associated with harpies is their penchant for stealing and hoarding shiny or valuable objects. In some legends, harpies are depicted as notorious thieves, snatching jewellery, coins, and other treasures to adorn their nests or decorate themselves. This behaviour is often attributed to their mischievous and cunning nature, as well as their attraction to items that glitter and catch the light.

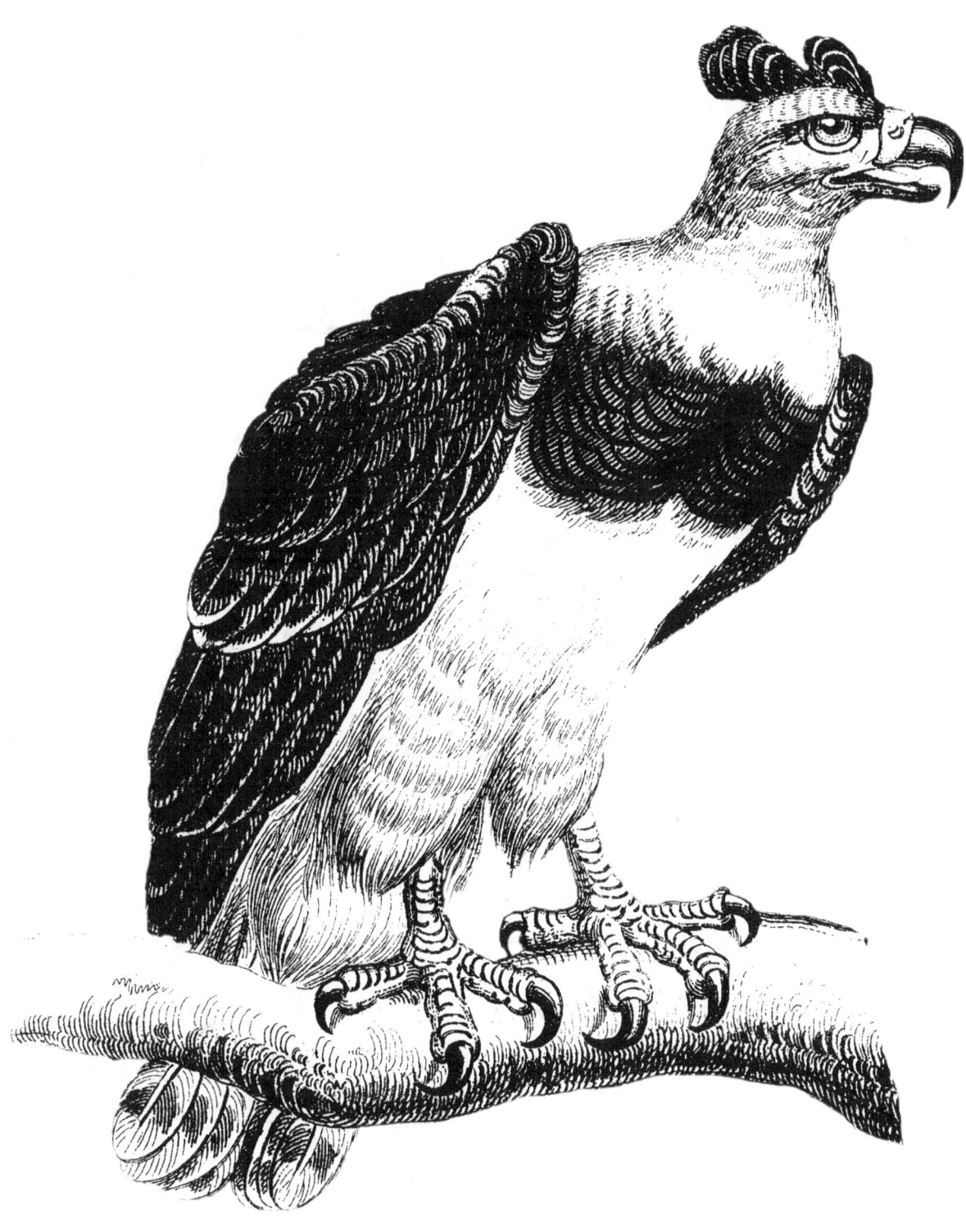

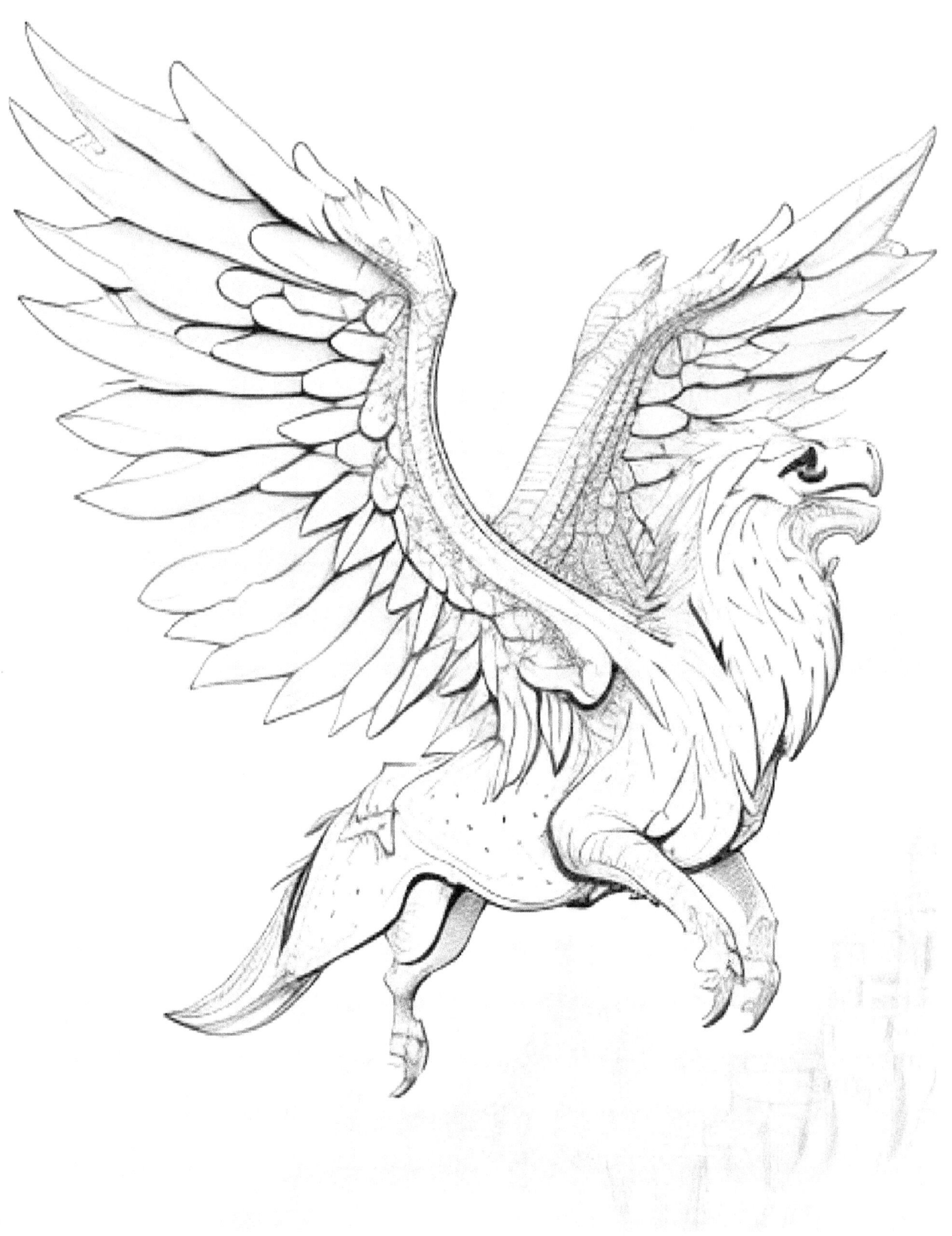

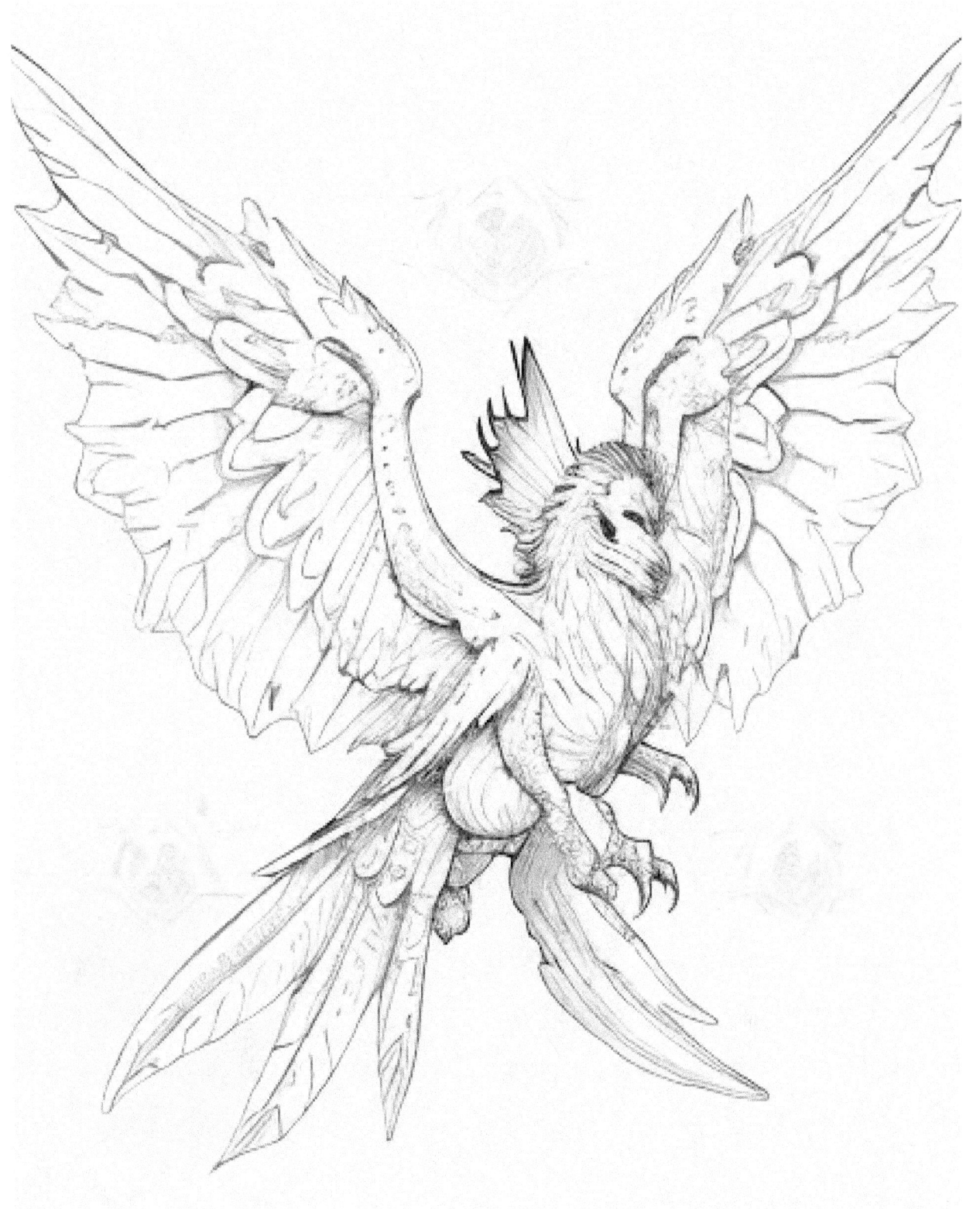

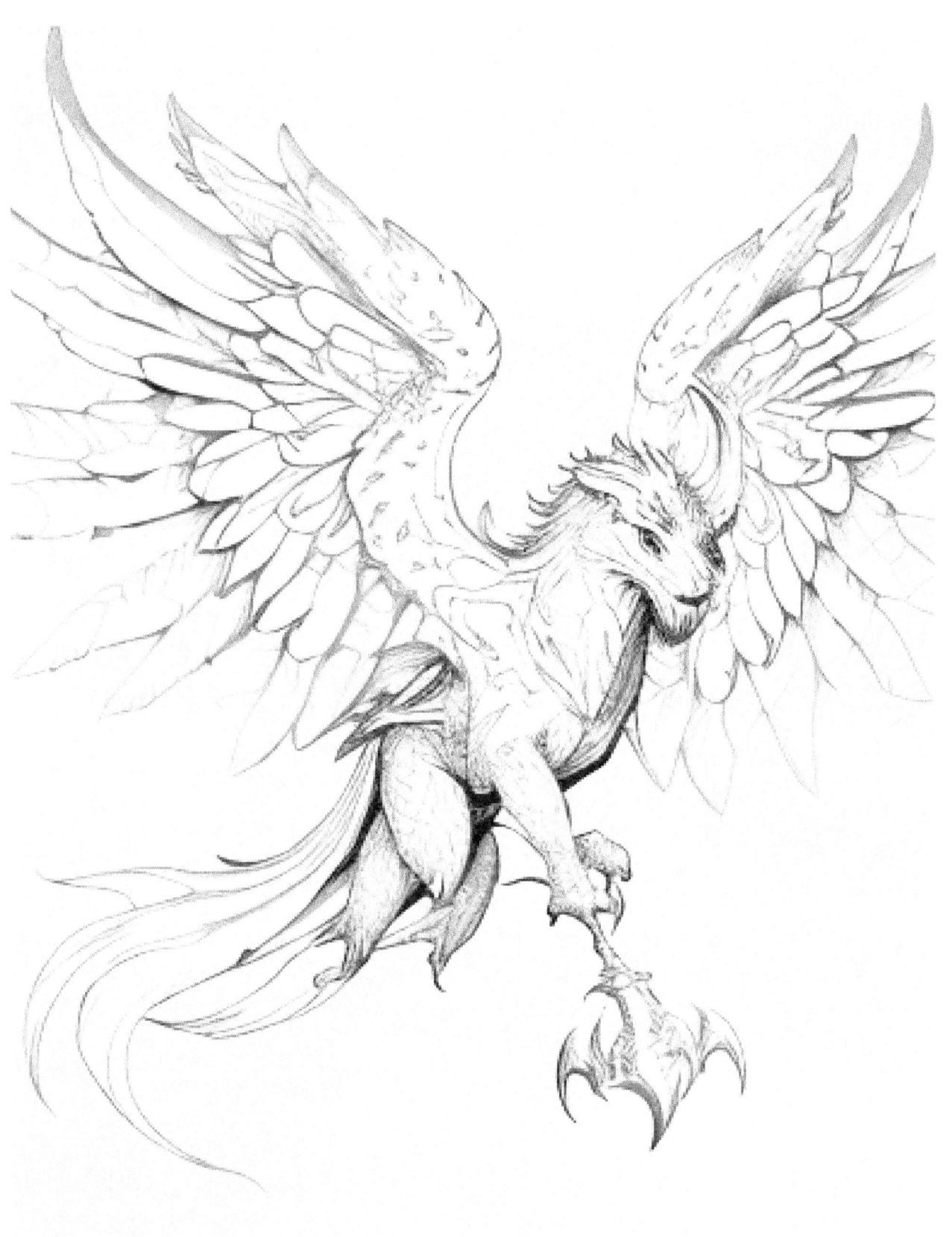

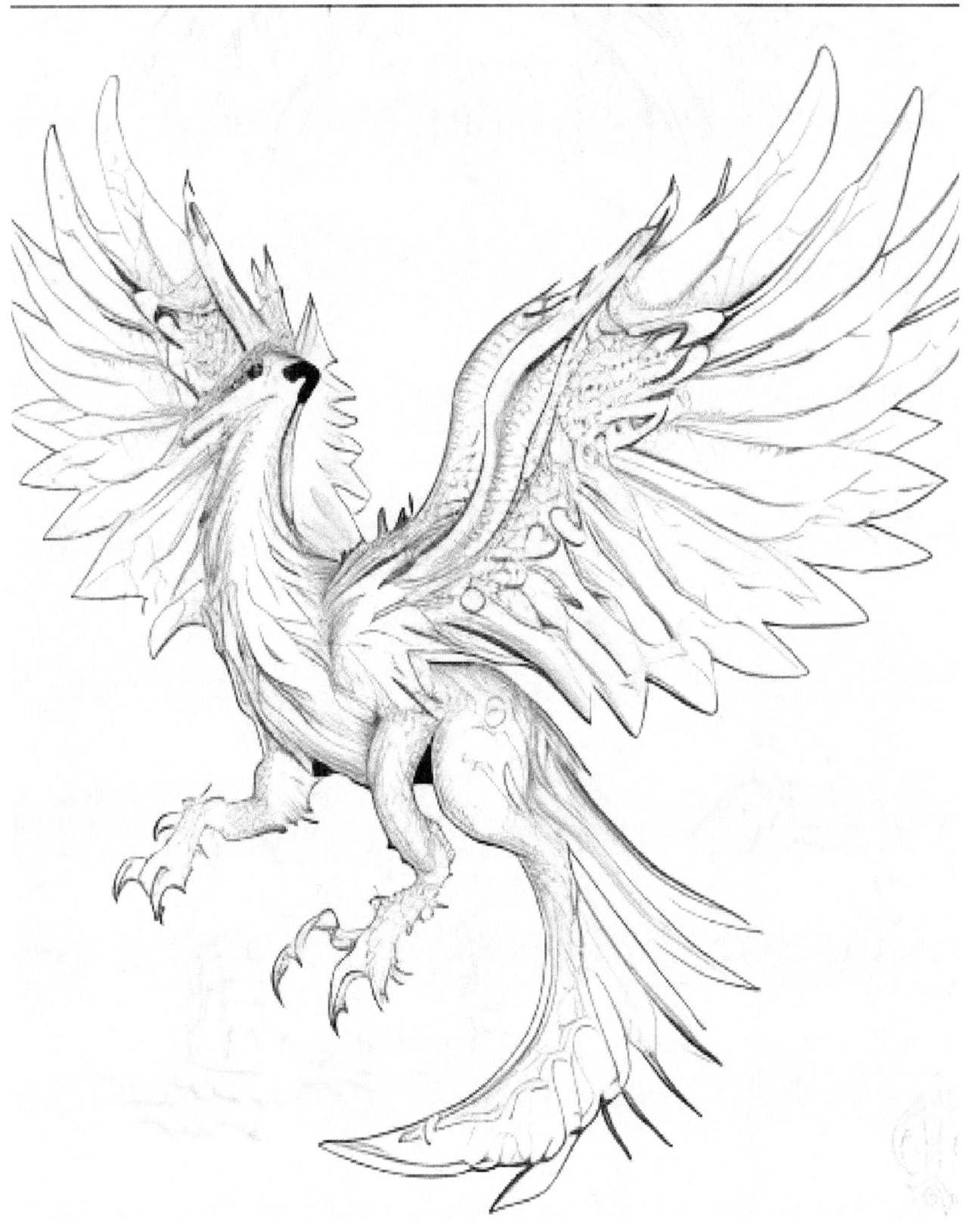

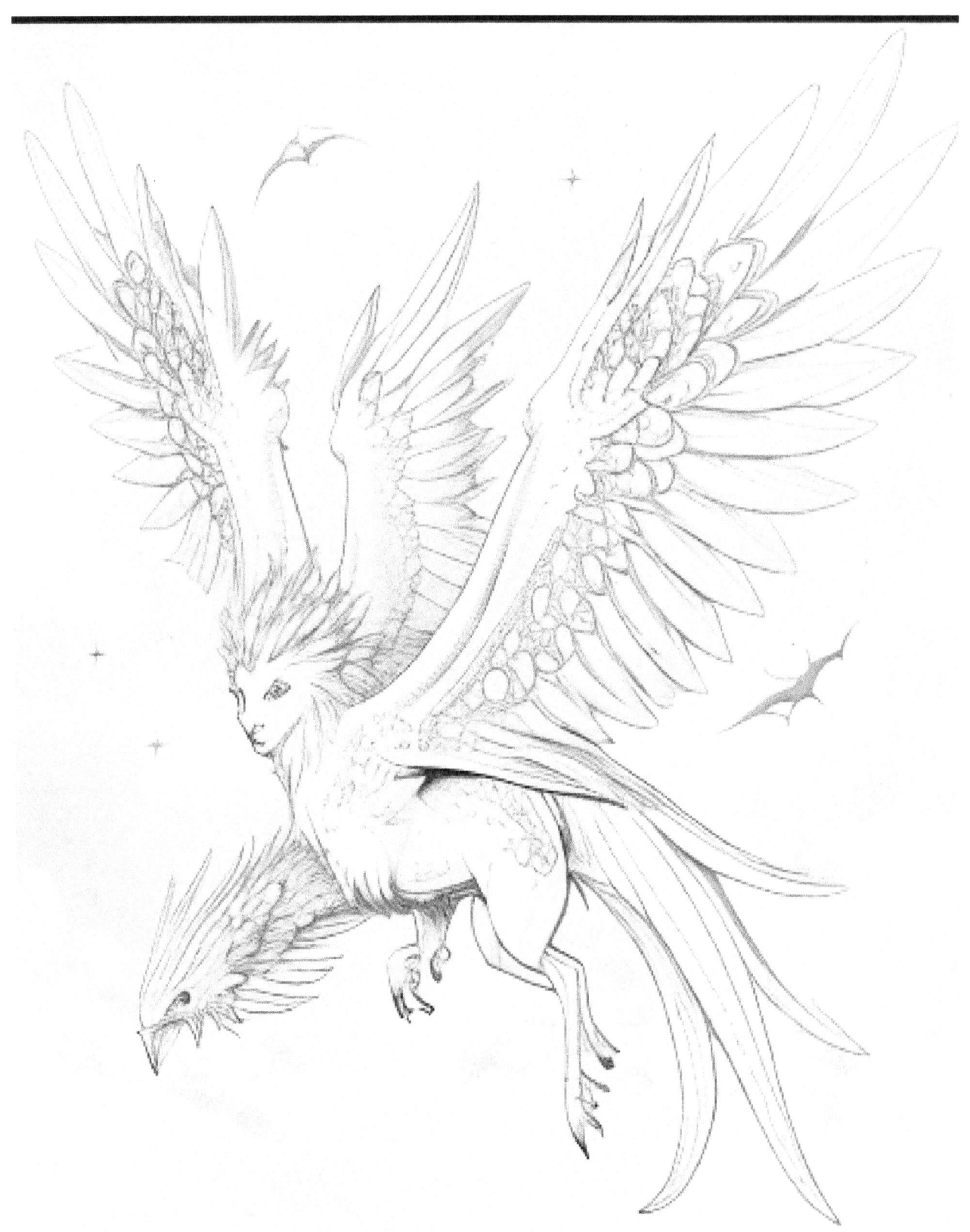

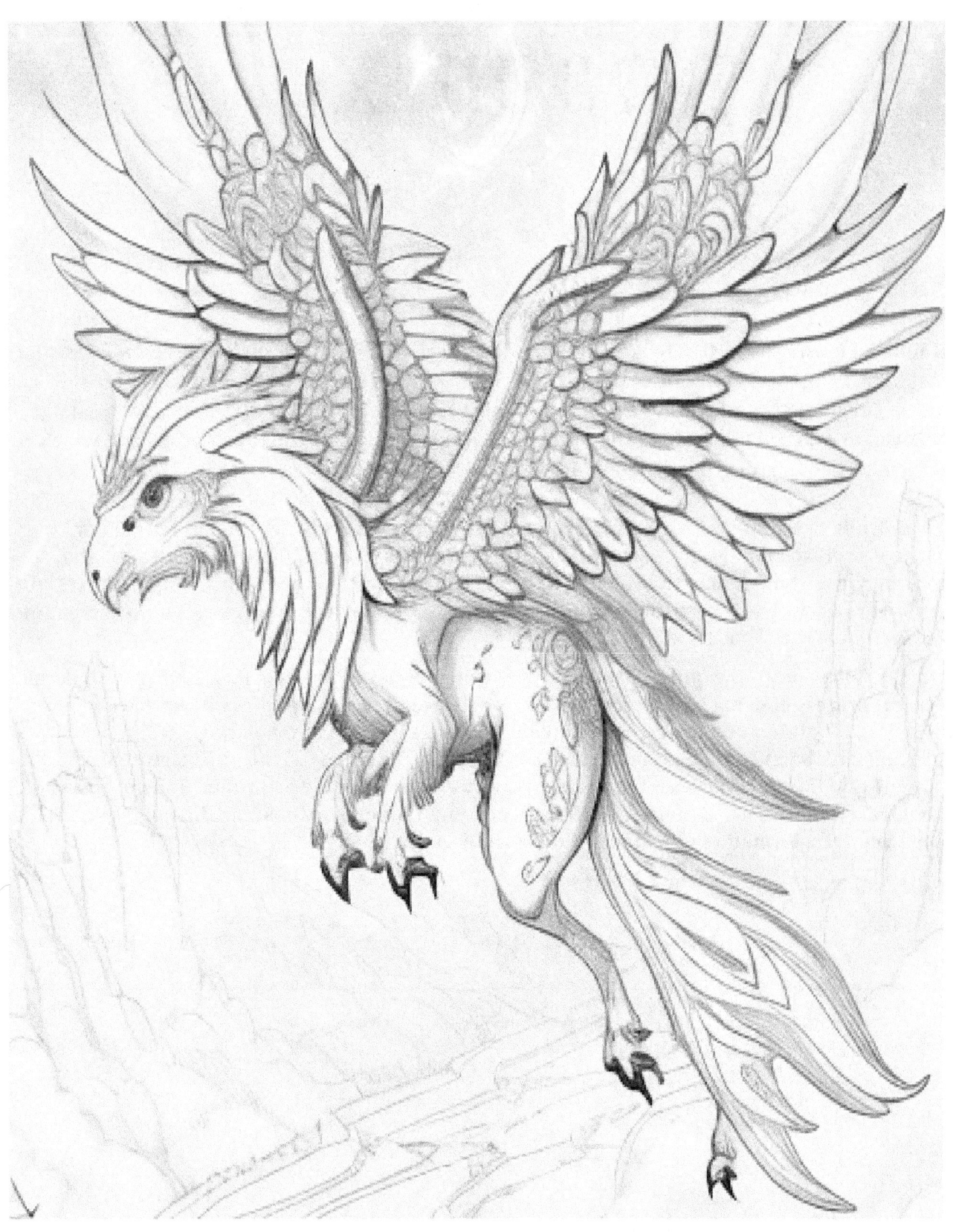

phoenix

Habitat: Phoenixes are said to inhabit remote and secluded habitats, such as deserts, forests, or mountain ranges. They are often associated with regions of intense heat and fire, where they can harness their elemental powers and find suitable materials for their nests. Phoenixes are believed to construct their nests from aromatic branches, such as cinnamon or myrrh, which they collect and arrange meticulously in their chosen habitat.

Food: Unlike other mythical creatures, phoenixes are not typically depicted as hunters or carnivores. Instead, they are said to sustain themselves on a diet of dewdrops and sunlight, drawing nourishment directly from the natural elements around them. This unique dietary preference adds to the mystical and ethereal qualities attributed to phoenixes, emphasizing their connection to the elements of fire and light.

Quirky Behaviour: One quirky behaviour associated with phoenixes is their ability to undergo a cyclical process of death and rebirth. According to legend, when a phoenix nears the end of its life cycle, it builds a nest of aromatic branches and sets it ablaze, immolating itself in a spectacular display of fire. From the ashes of this fiery funeral pyre, a new phoenix emerges, symbolizing the eternal cycle of death and renewal. This dramatic behaviour underscores the mythical creature's association with resurrection and immortality, making it a potent symbol of hope and transformation in various cultural traditions.

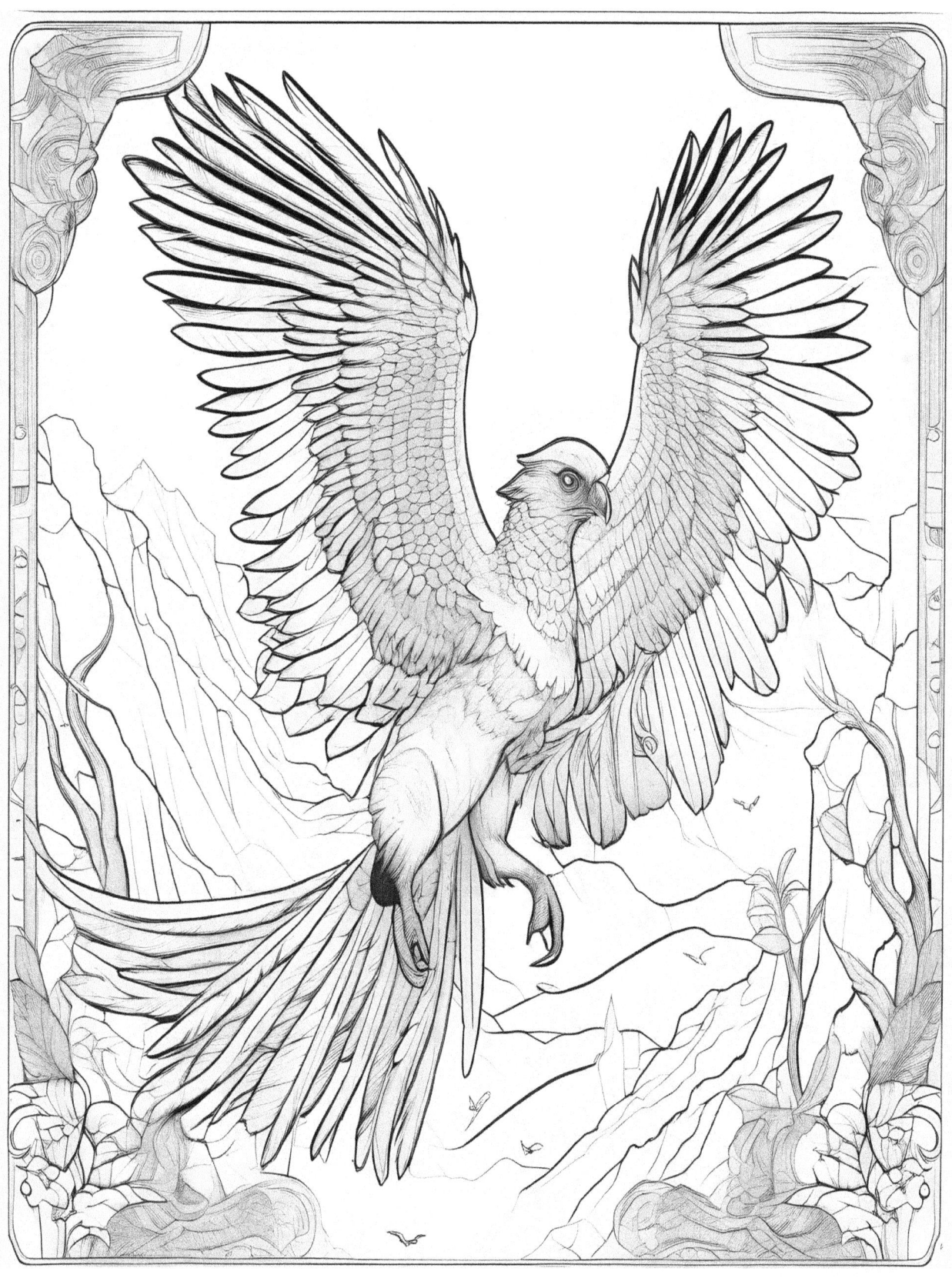

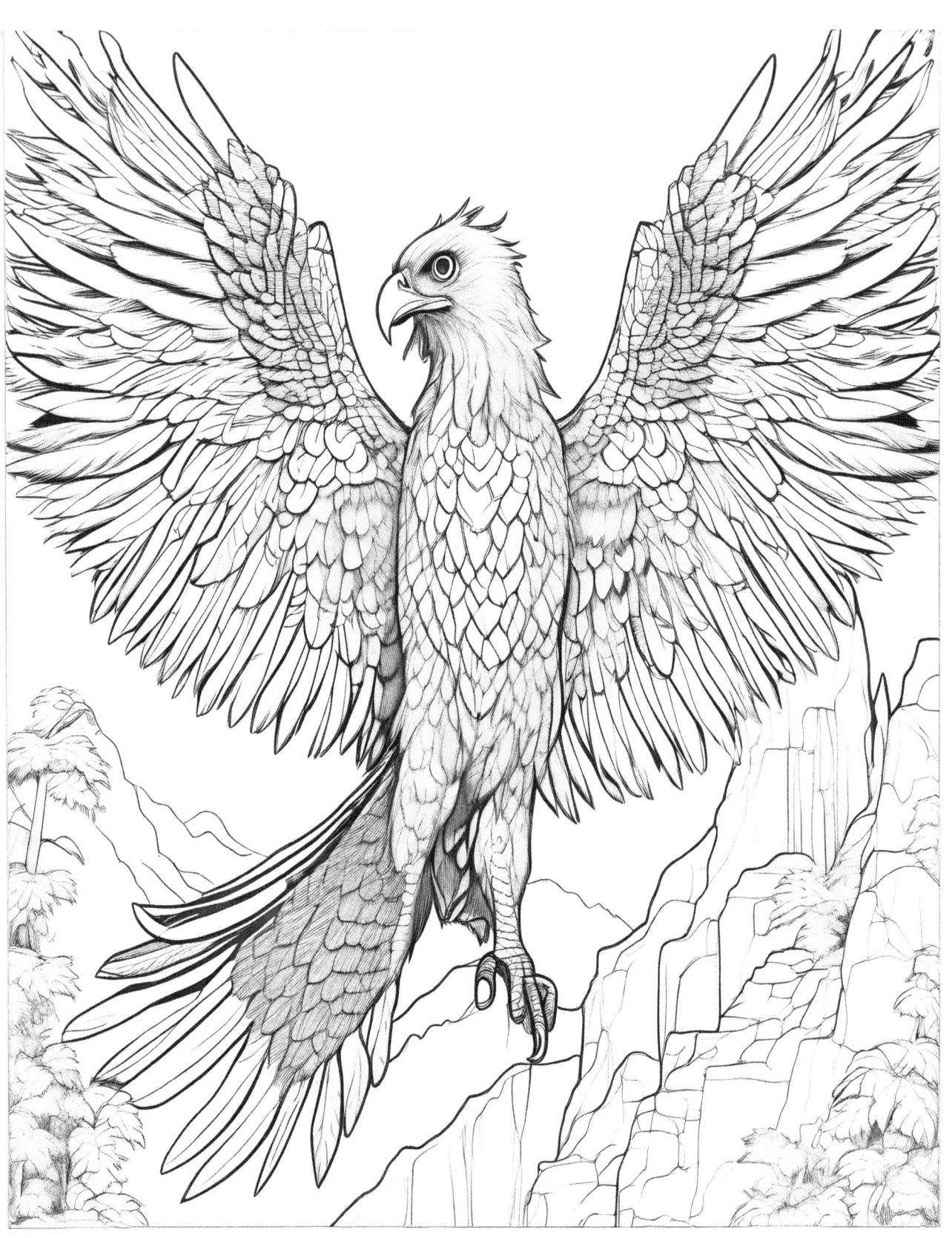

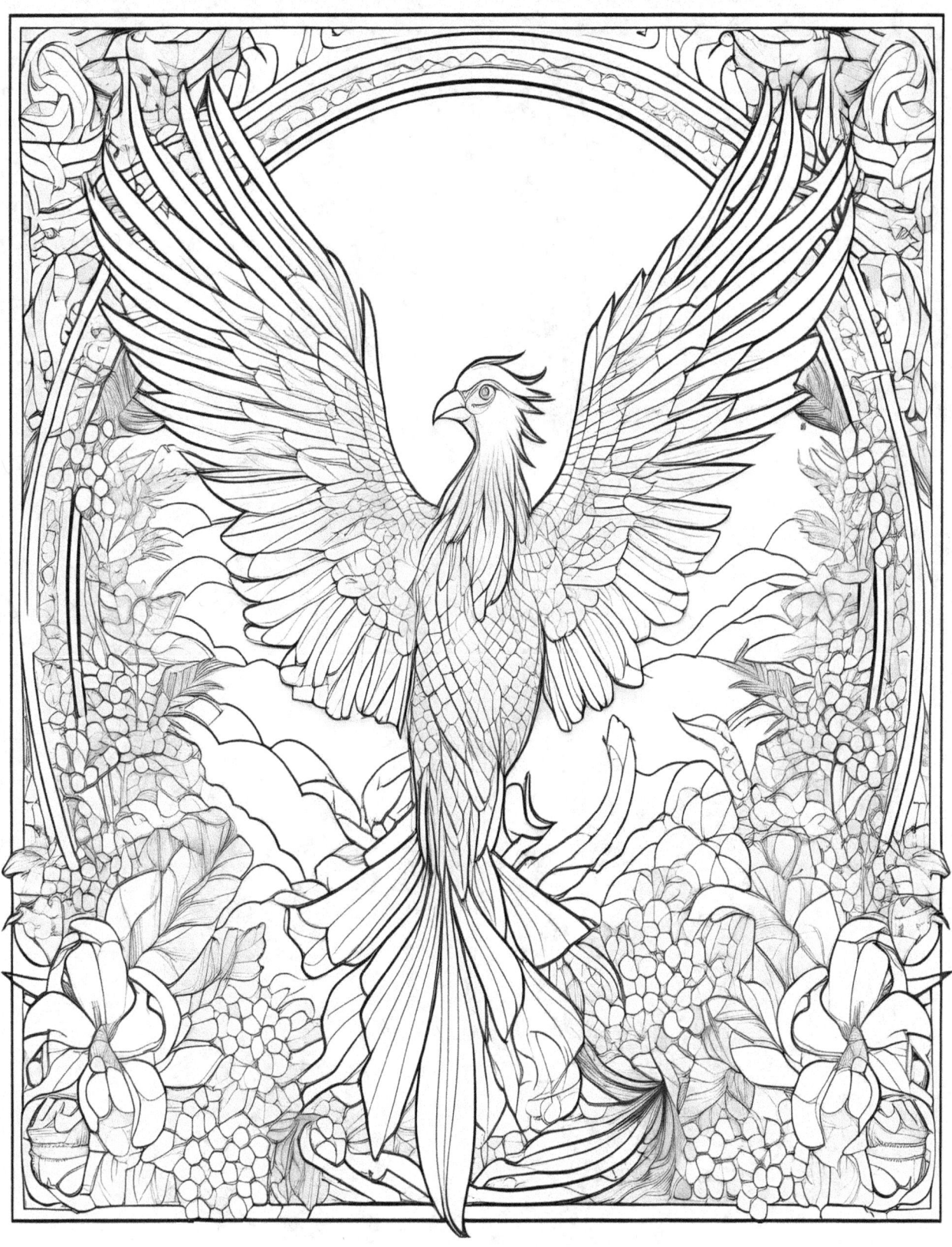

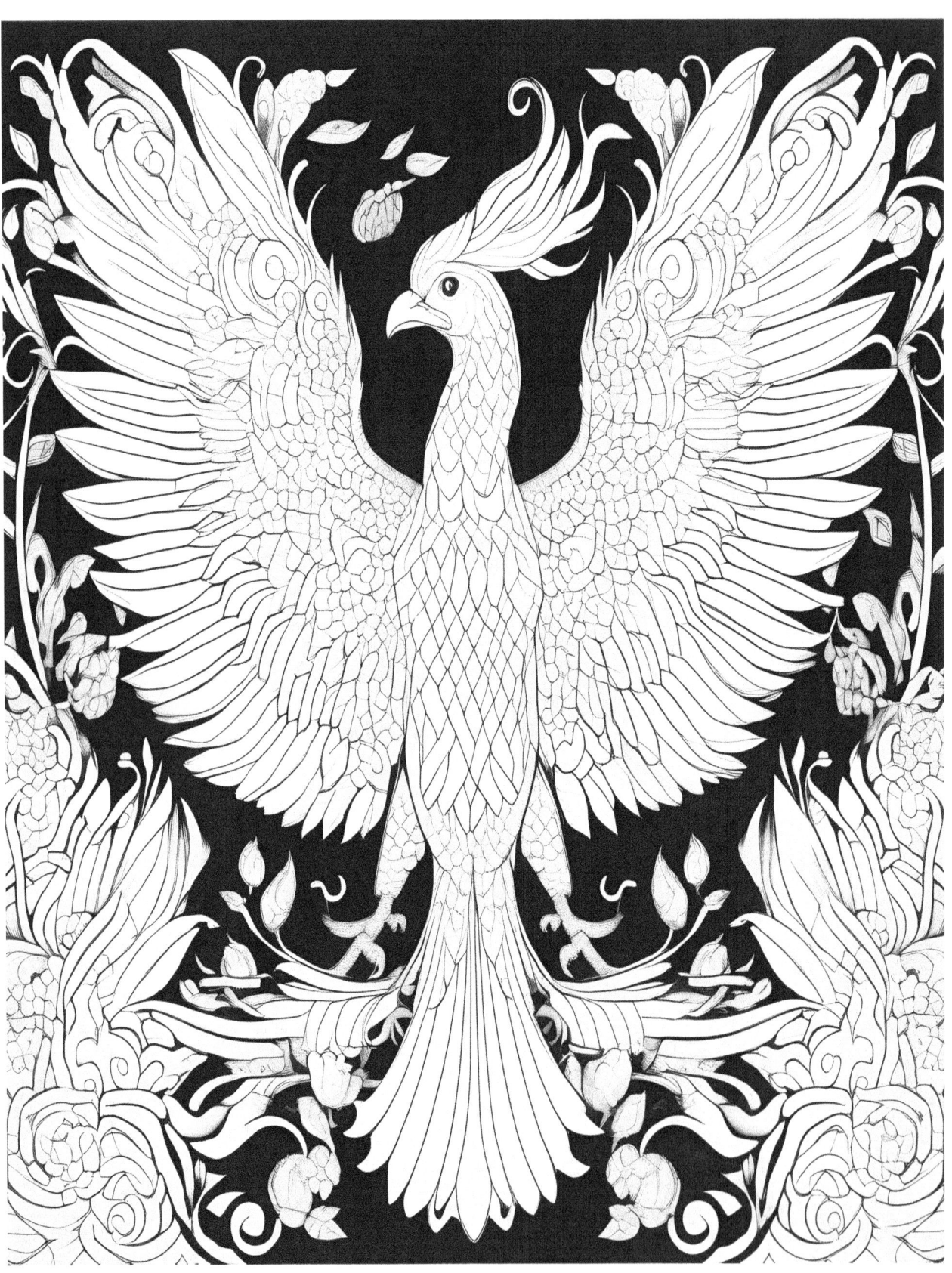

Lions

Habitat: Lions inhabit a diverse range of habitats, including grasslands, savannas, scrub forests, and semi-arid regions. They prefer areas with access to water sources and sufficient cover for hunting and resting. Pride territories can vary greatly in size, from a few square miles to over 100 square miles, depending on factors such as prey availability and competition with other lion prides.

Food: As apex predators, lions primarily prey on large herbivores such as zebras, wildebeests, buffalo, and antelopes. Lionesses are the primary hunters in the pride, employing coordinated tactics to stalk and ambush their prey. After a successful hunt, lions gorge themselves on the fresh kill, often consuming large quantities of meat in a single feeding session. Lions are opportunistic feeders and will scavenge on carcasses abandoned by other predators when the opportunity arises.

Quirky Behaviour: One quirky behaviour of lions is their fondness for socializing and displaying affection within their pride. Lions are highly social animals, living in family groups called prides typically consisting of related females, their offspring, and a coalition of dominant males. Within the pride, lions engage in grooming, playful interactions, and communal resting, strengthening social bonds and reinforcing their cooperative hunting strategies. Another quirky behaviour observed in some lion prides is all parenting, where lionesses nurse and care for the cubs of other females within the pride, promoting group cohesion and ensuring the survival of all offspring.

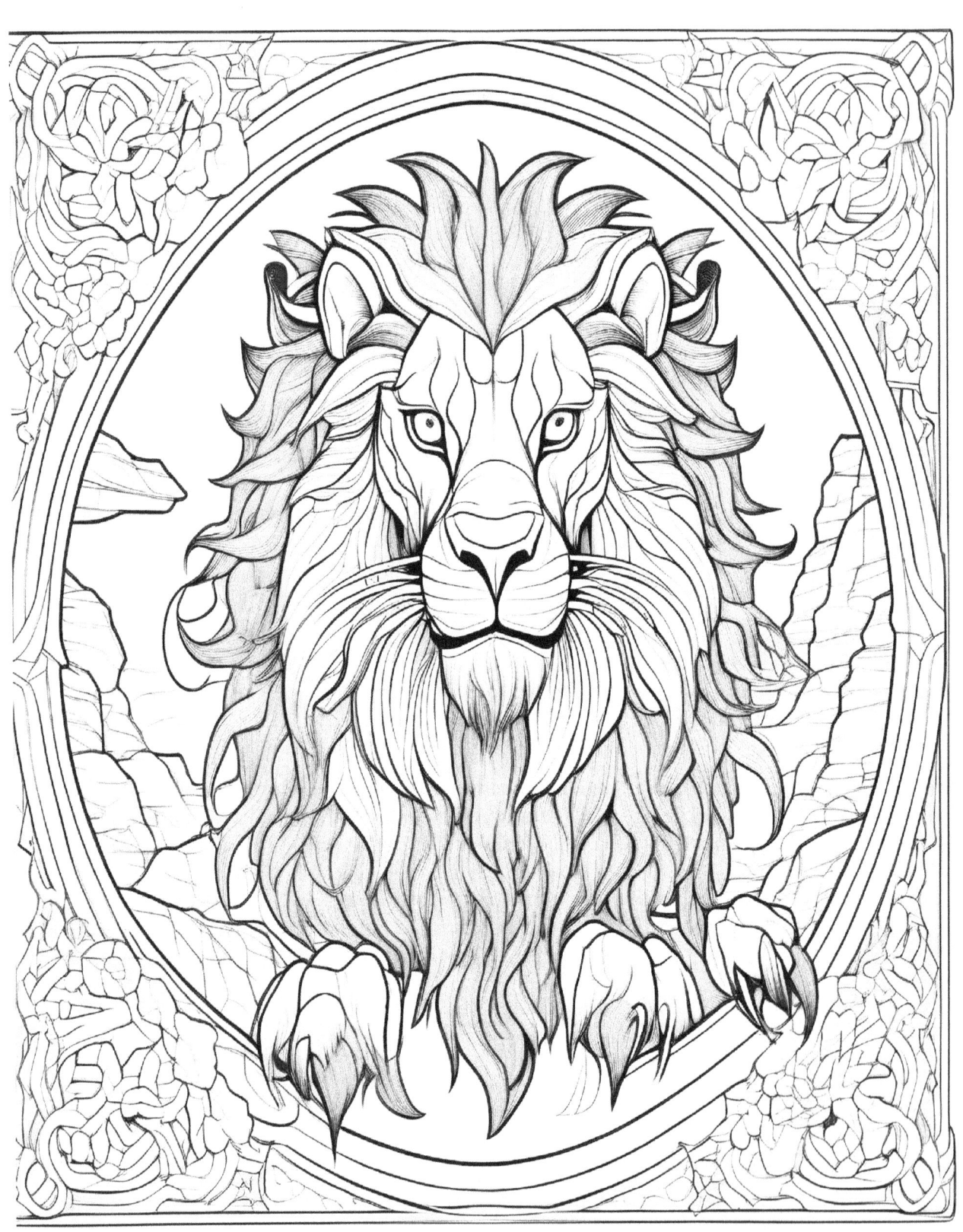

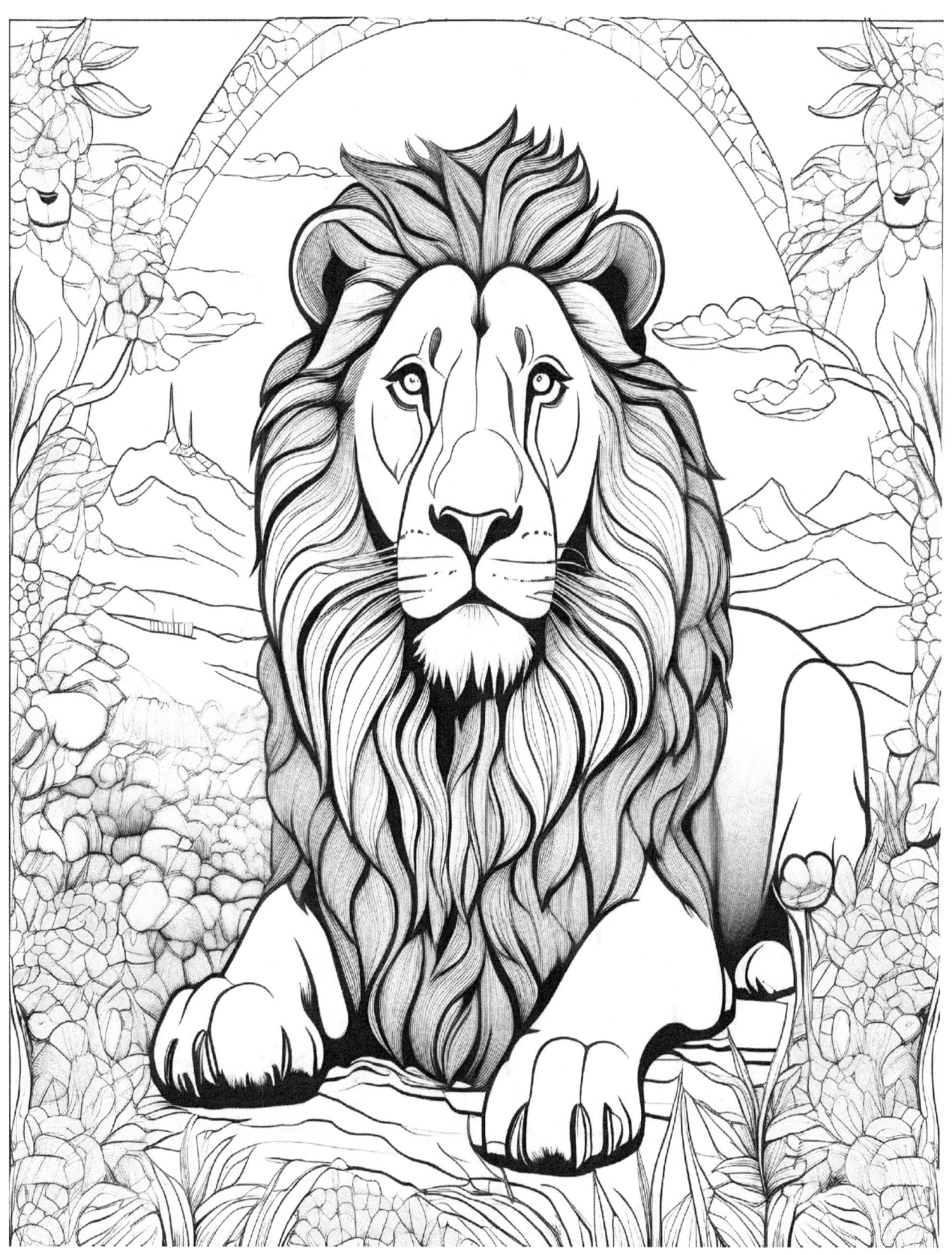

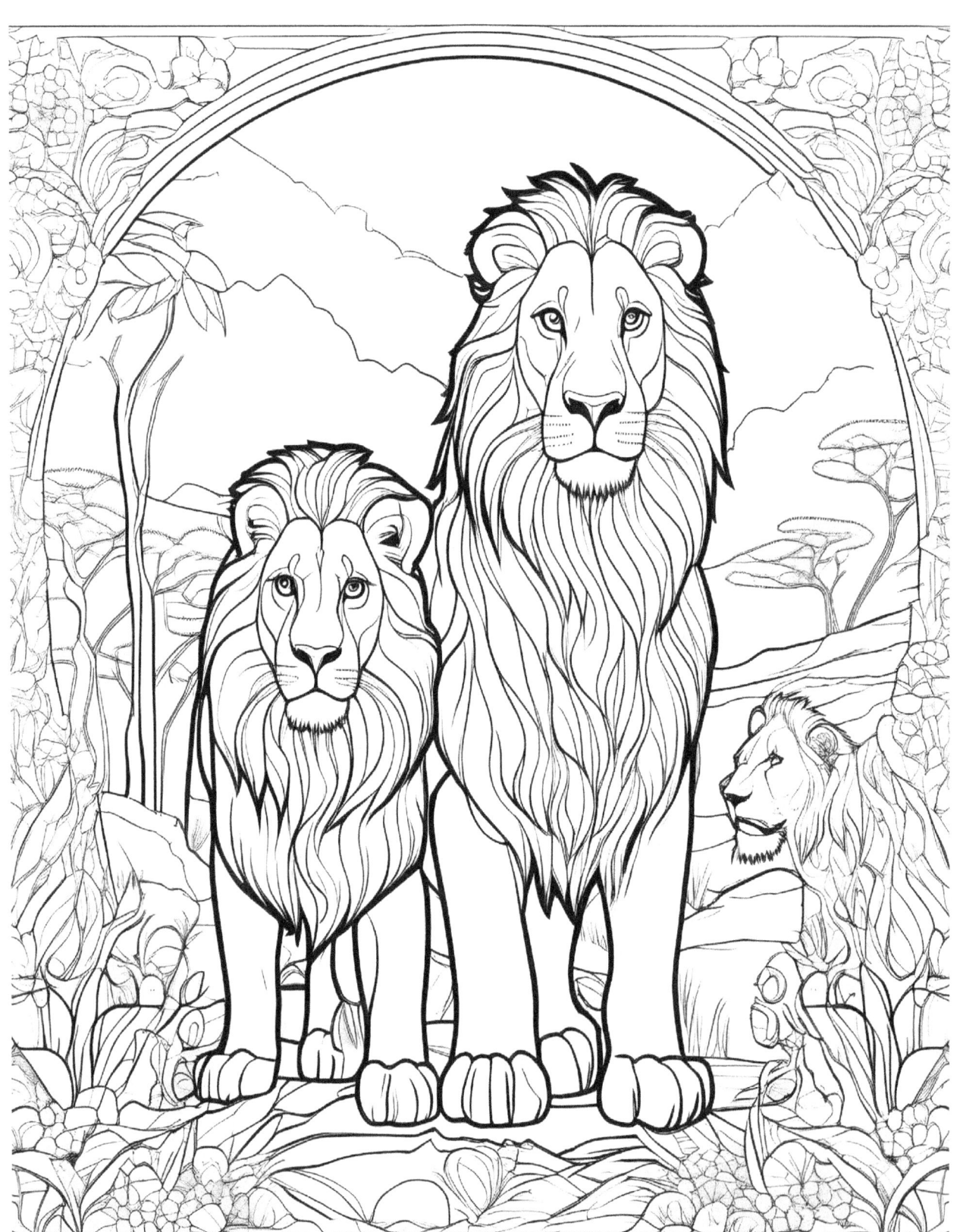

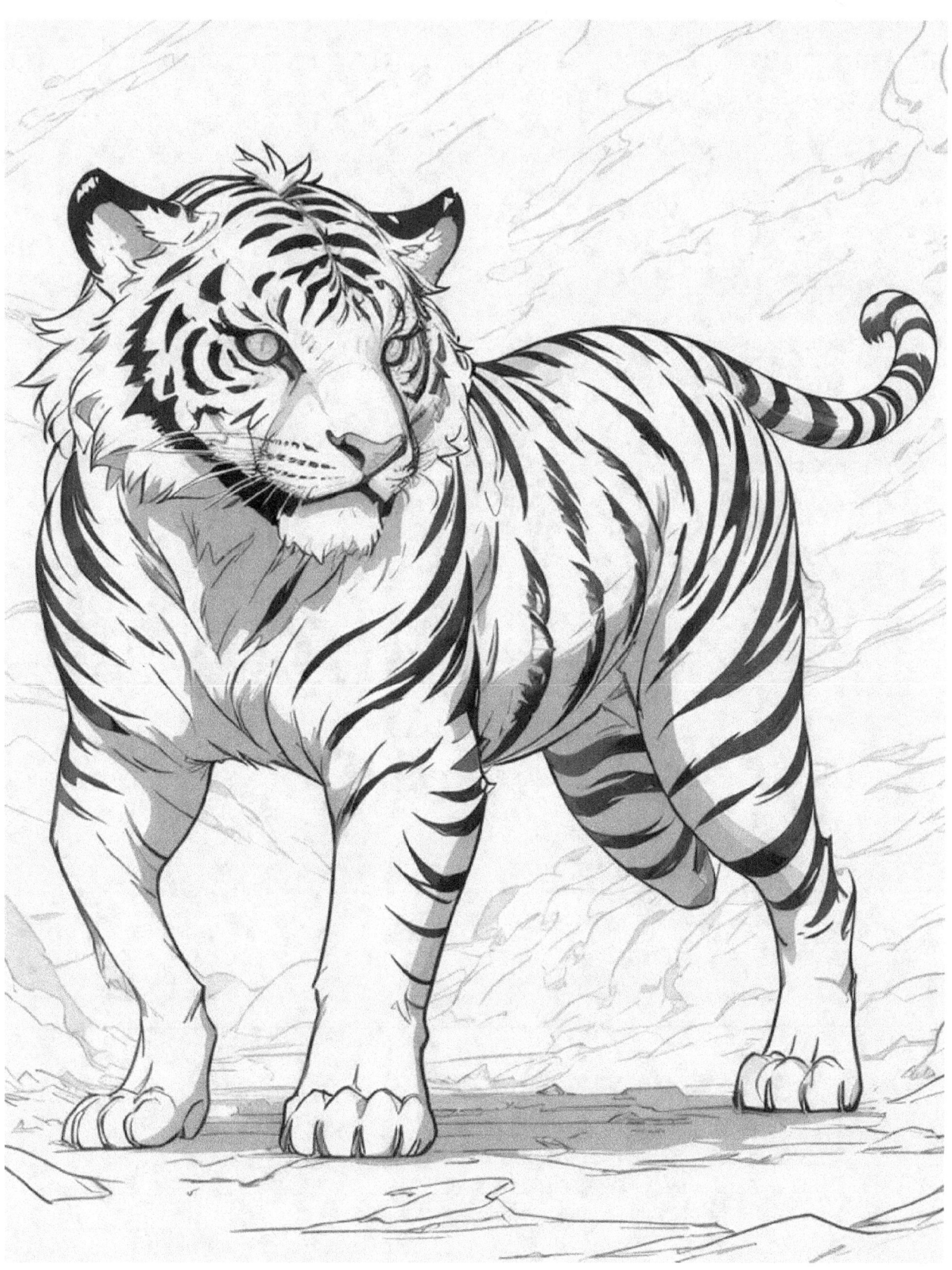

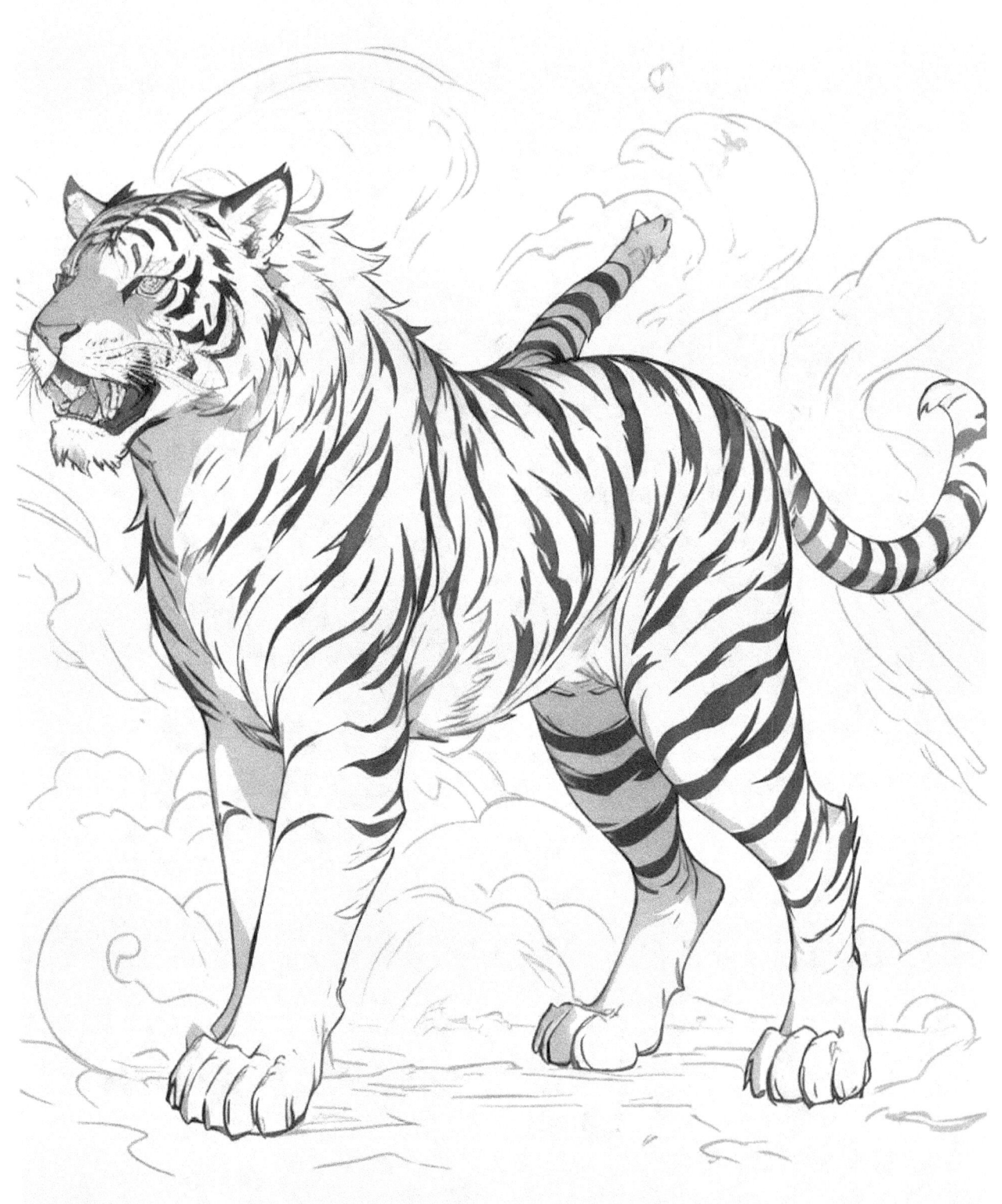

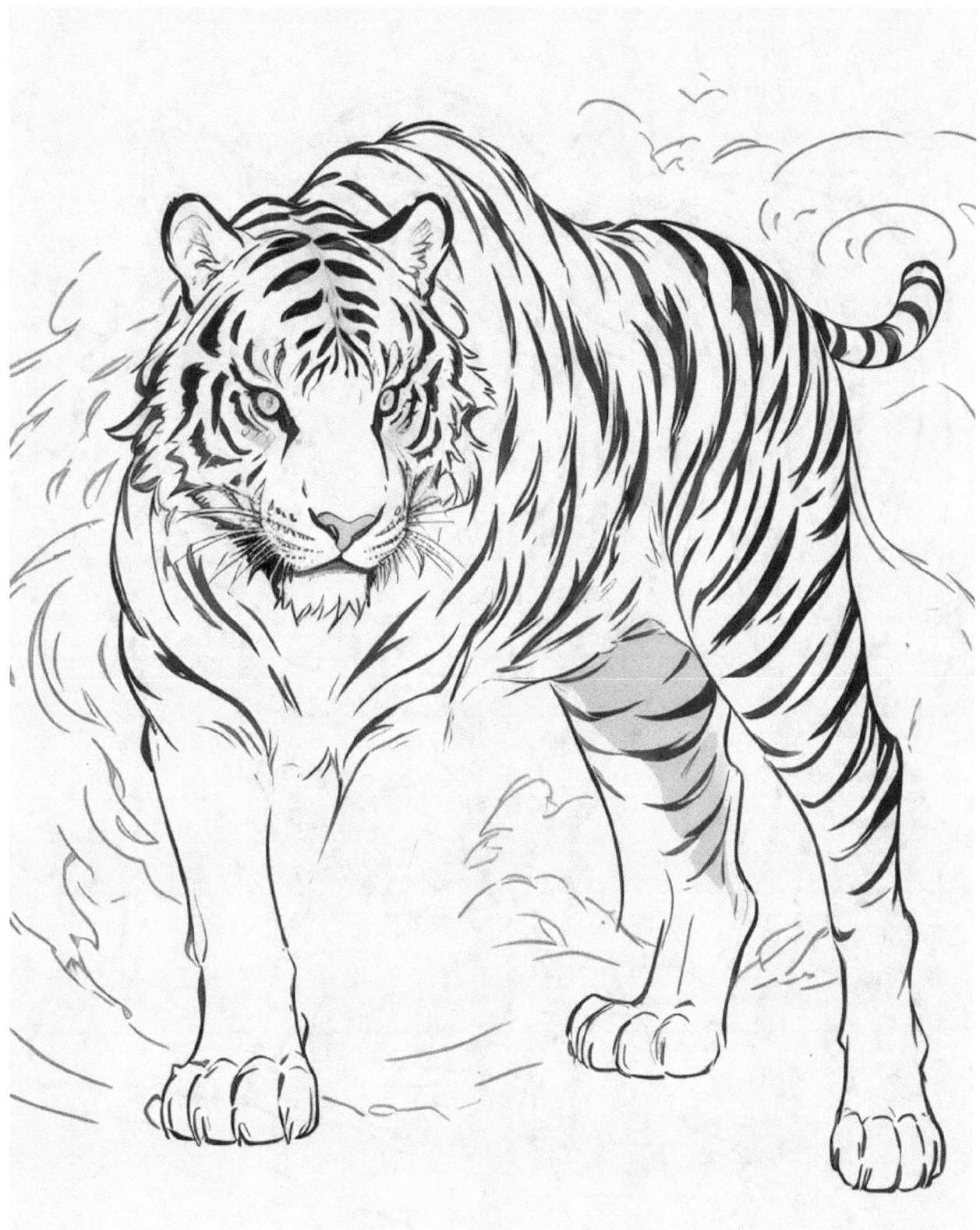

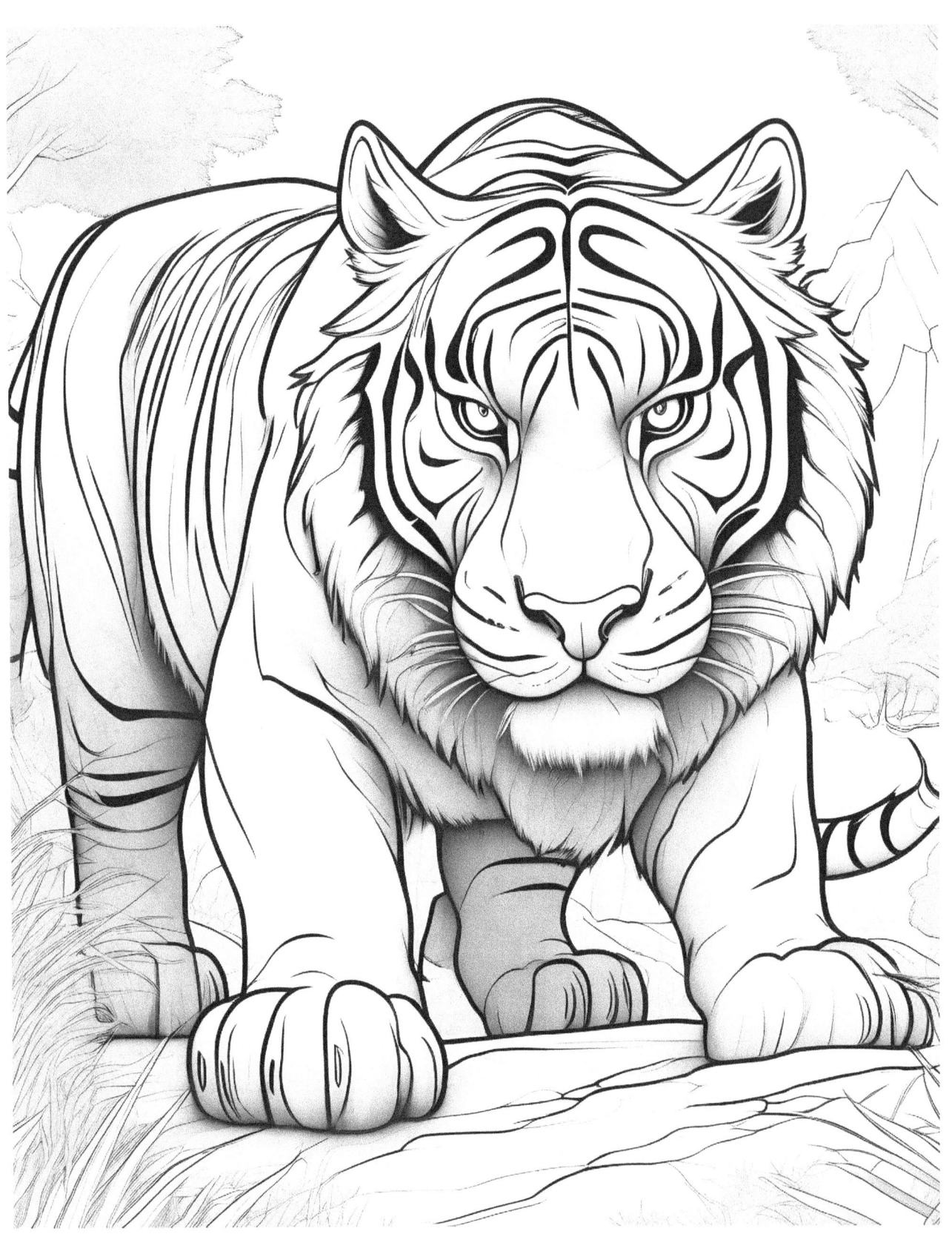

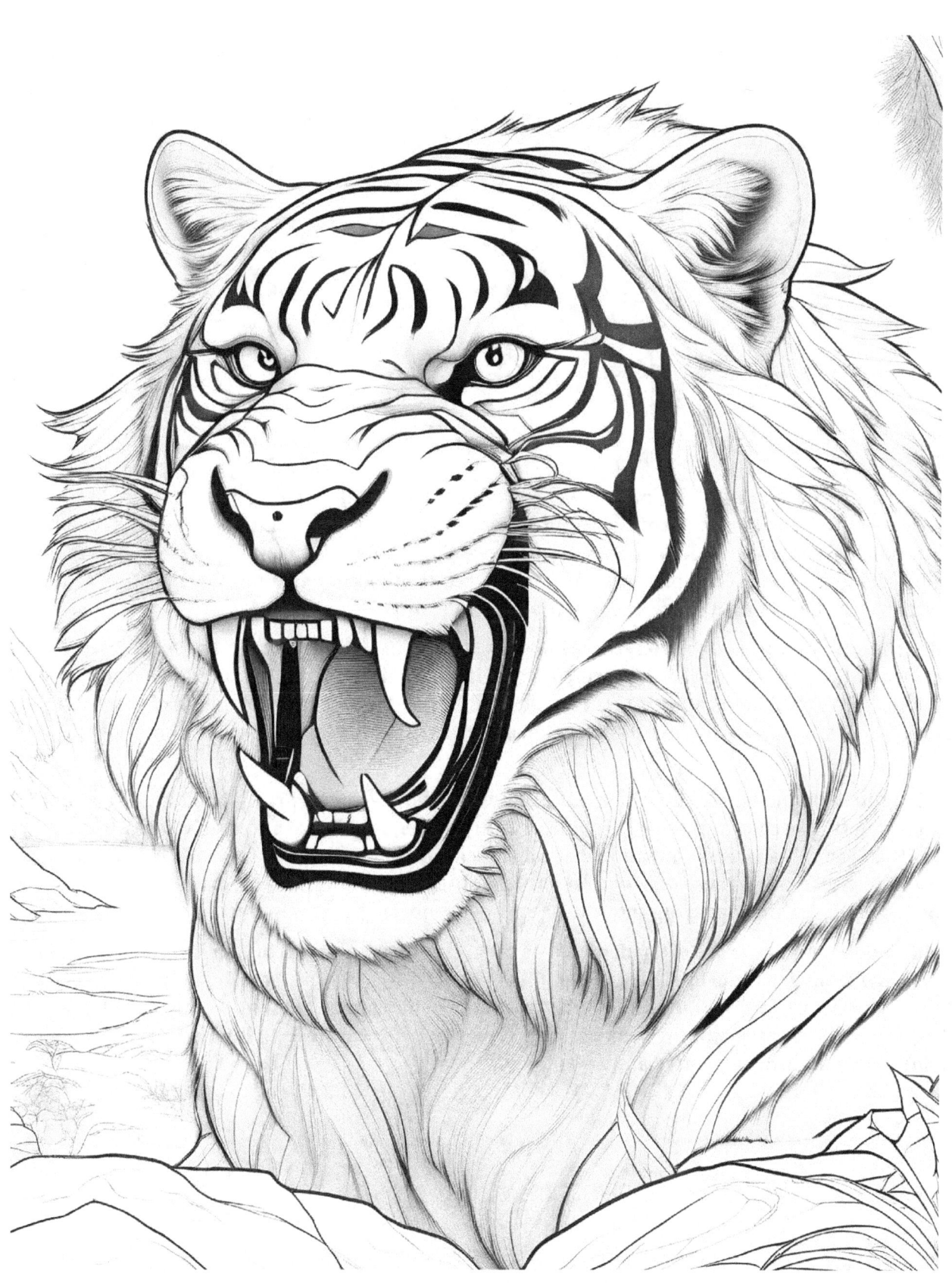

Habitat: Unicorns are said to inhabit enchanted forests, lush meadows, and other idyllic landscapes filled with abundant flora and fauna. These mythical creatures are often associated with magical realms or hidden dimensions, where they roam freely among ancient groves and shimmering streams. The unicorn's habitat reflects its ethereal nature and connection to the natural world, evoking a sense of wonder and tranquility.

Food: In folklore, unicorns are believed to subsist on a diet of pure water, fresh grasses, and the essence of flowers. They are often depicted grazing peacefully in sun-dappled meadows or drinking from crystal-clear springs. The purity of their diet mirrors the unicorn's symbolic association with innocence and untainted beauty, emphasizing their ethereal and otherworldly qualities.

Quirky Behaviour: One quirky behaviour often attributed to unicorns is their elusive and solitary nature. According to legend, unicorns are exceedingly rare and elusive creatures, preferring to dwell in remote and inaccessible locations far from human civilization. They are said to possess a keen sense of intuition and are able to evade capture through their innate magical abilities, disappearing into the depths of the forest at the slightest hint of danger.

Additionally, unicorns are often depicted as creatures of great wisdom and healing, with their horns possessing mystical properties capable of purifying water and curing ailments. In some folklore, unicorns are said to display playful and mischievous behaviour, luring travellers deeper into the forest with their enchanting presence before vanishing into the shadows, leaving behind only a sense of wonder and mystery.

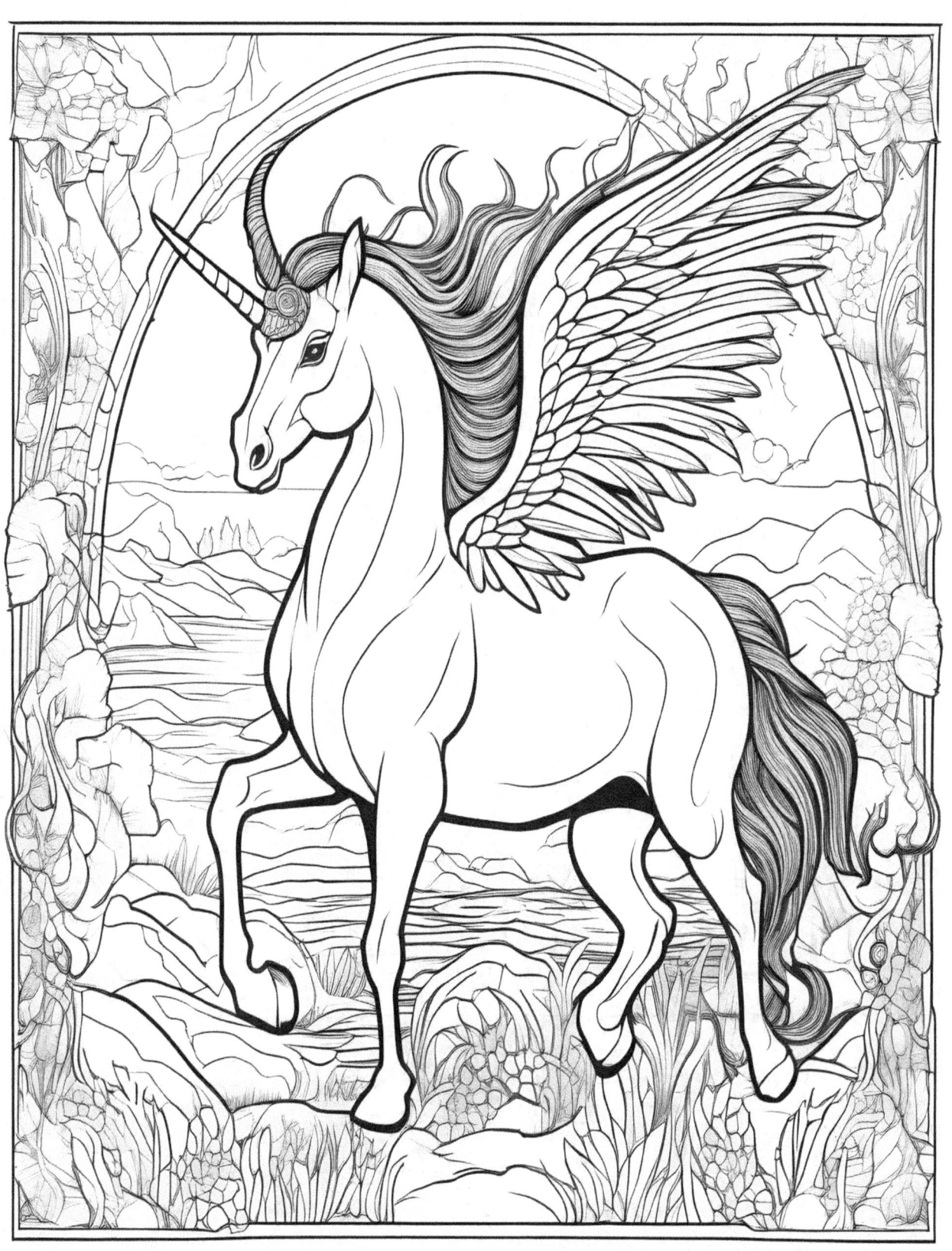

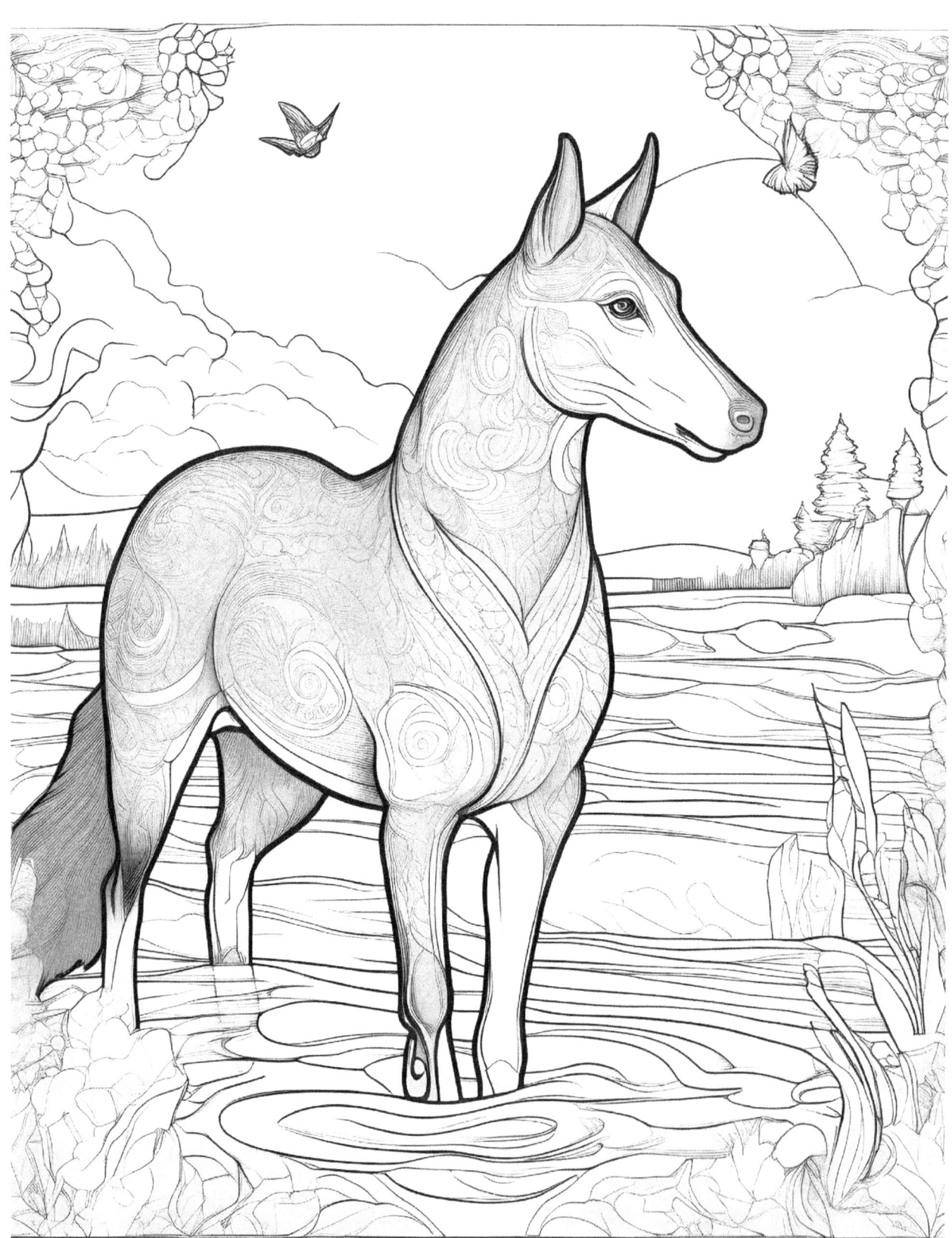

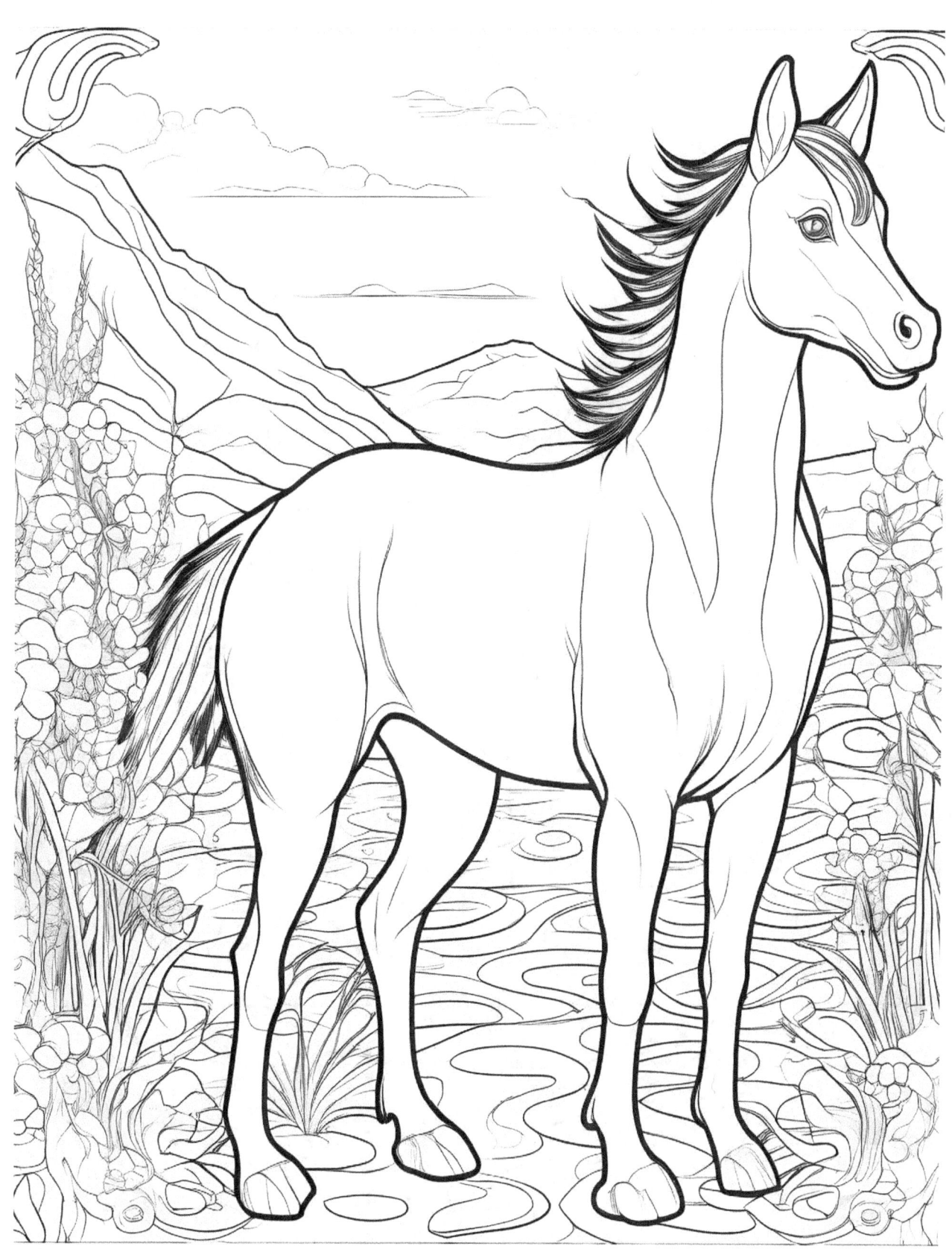

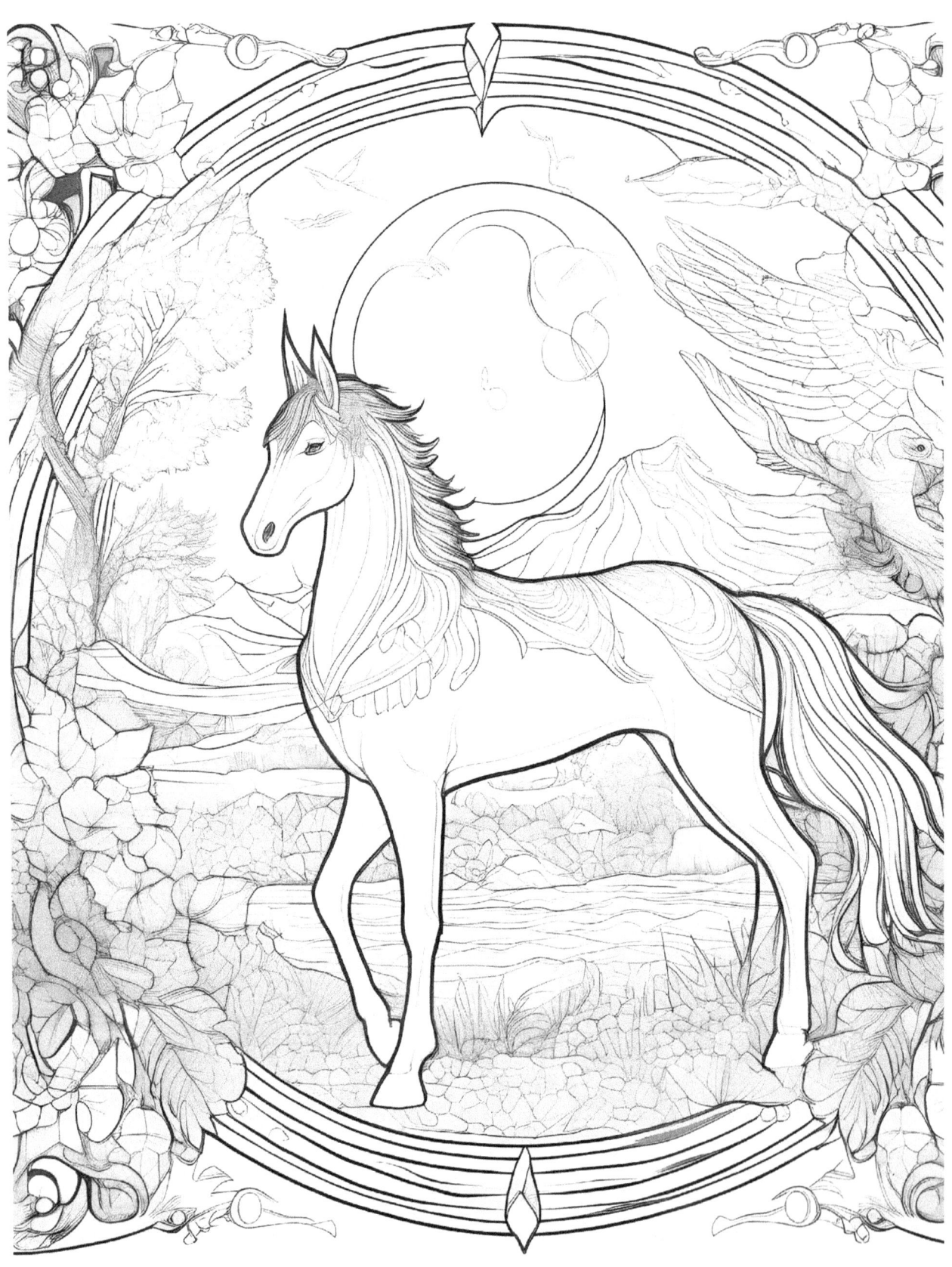

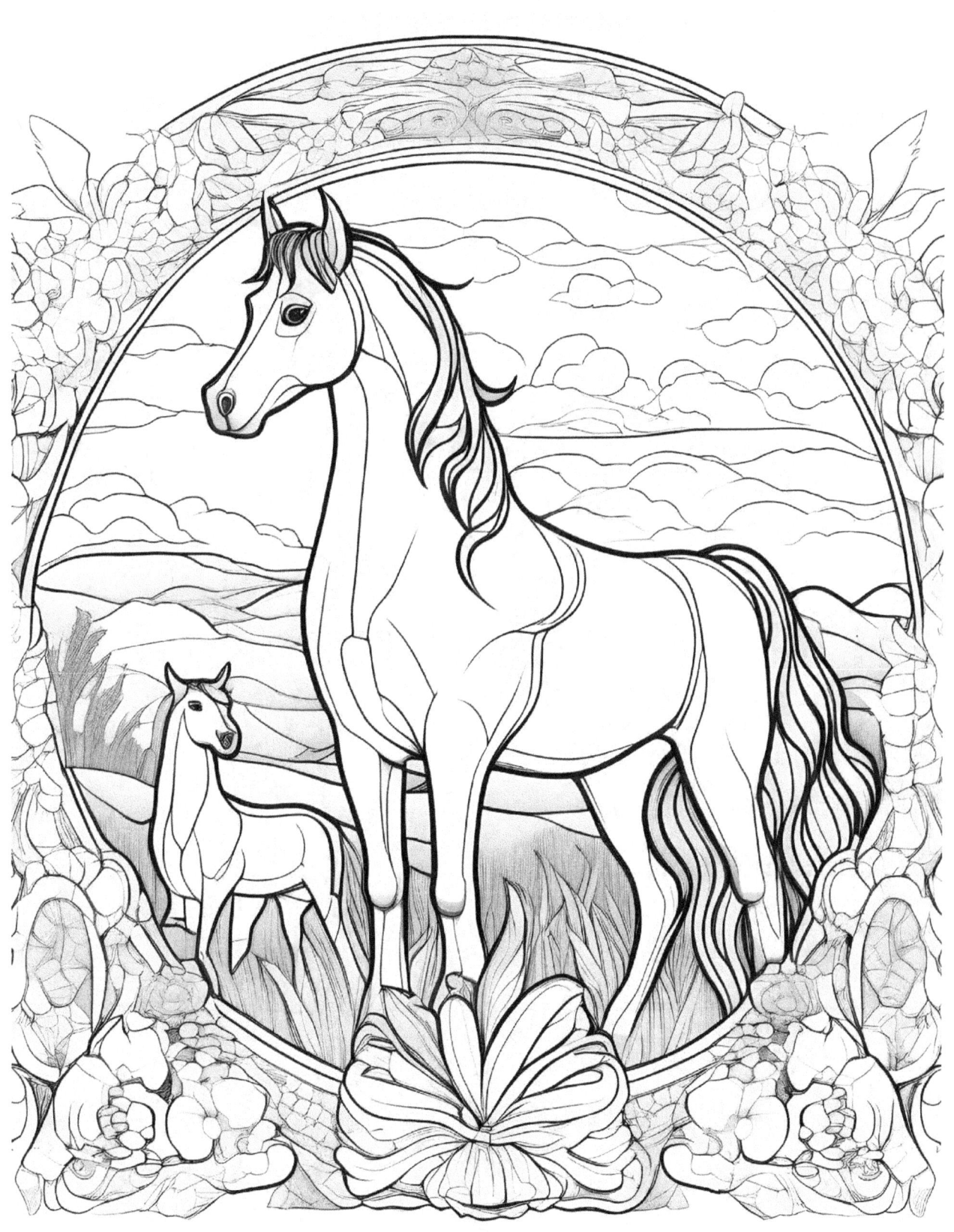

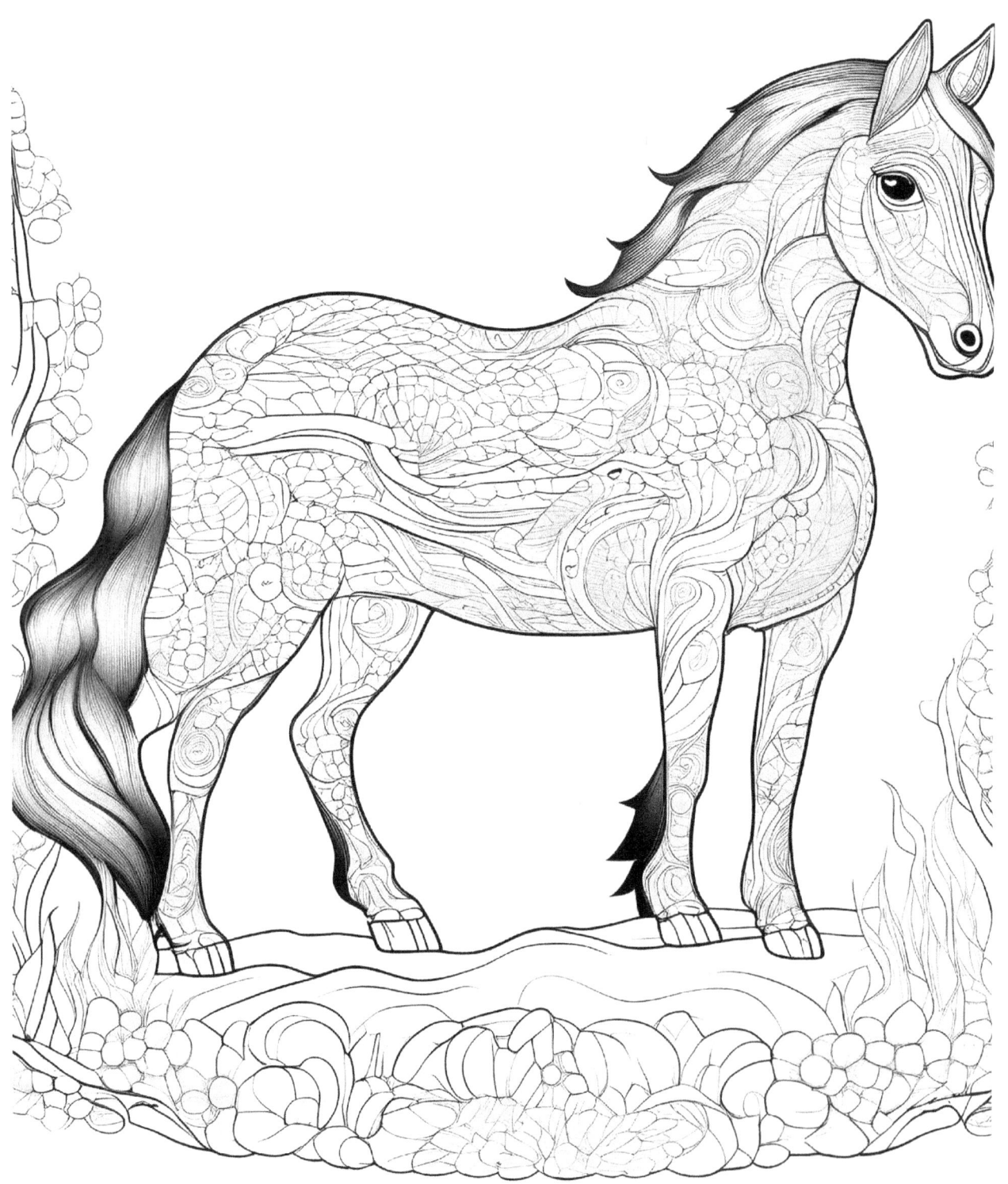

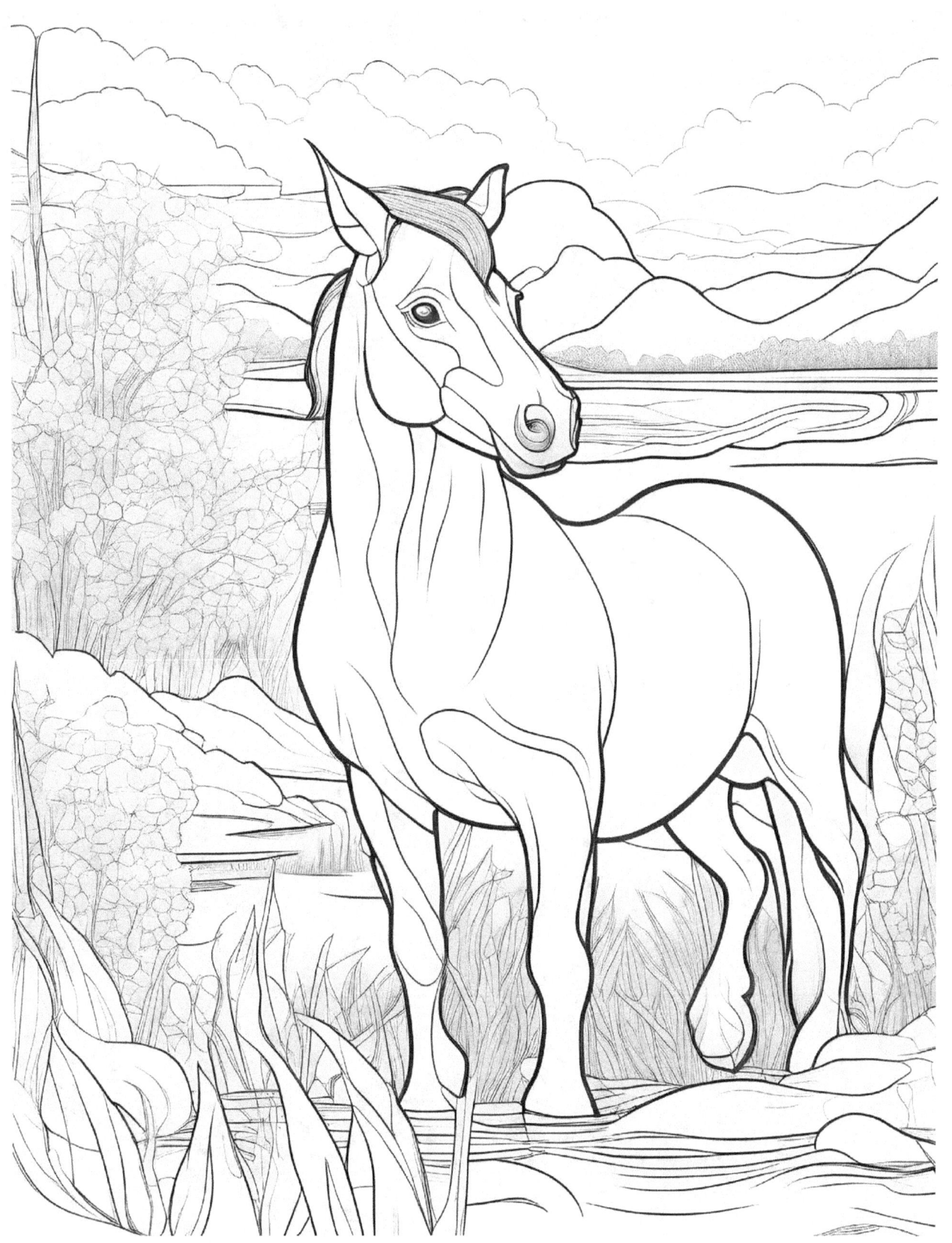

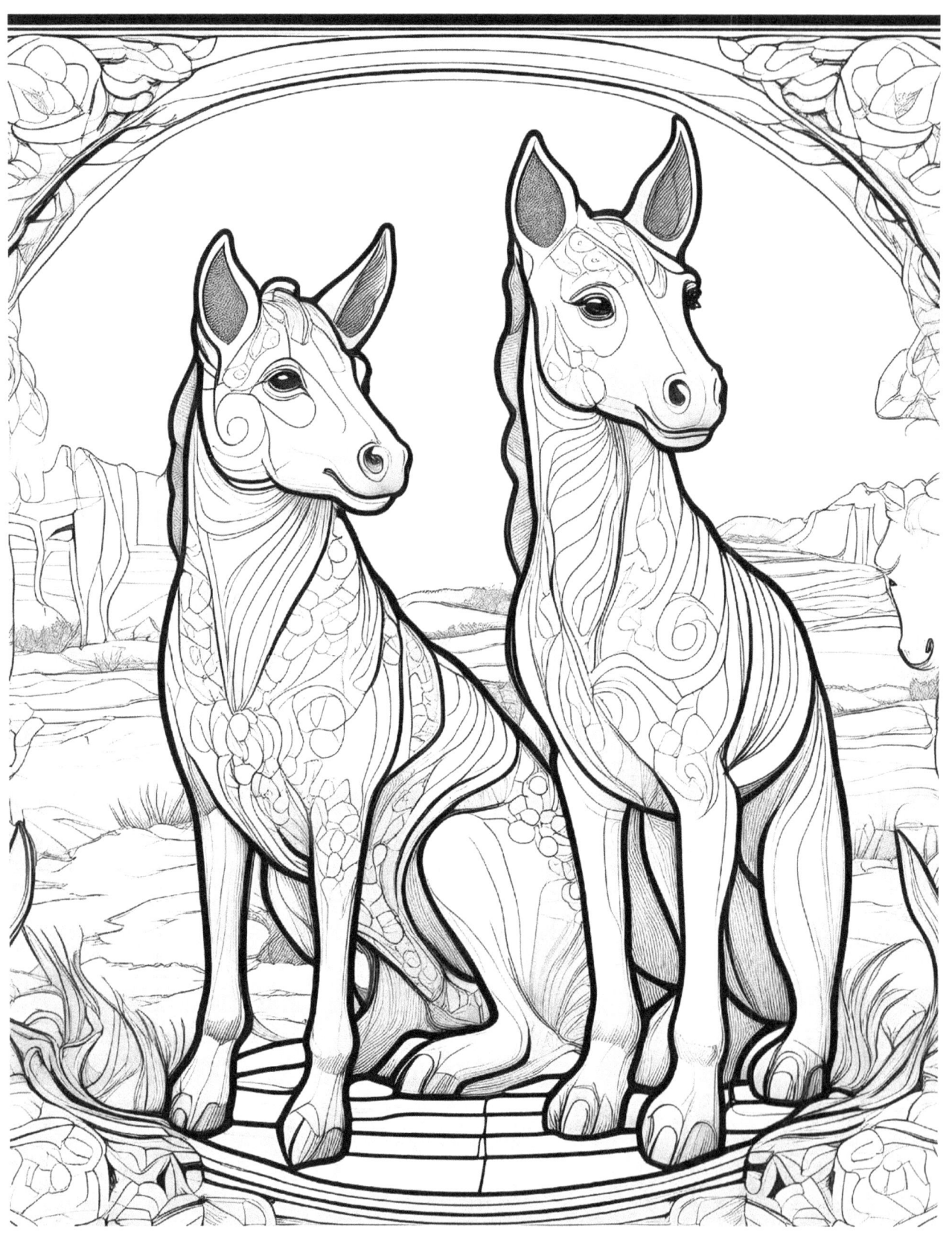

Mystical Creatures

Habitat: Mystical creatures are often associated with enchanted realms, mystical forests, and otherworldly landscapes beyond the ordinary realm of existence. They may inhabit hidden realms accessible only through magical gateways or dwell in remote and secluded locations far from human civilization. Their habitats are typically depicted as ethereal and otherworldly, filled with magical energies and fantastical landscapes that defy the laws of nature.

Food: The dietary preferences of mystical creatures vary widely depending on their cultural origins and mythological attributes. Some mystical creatures, such as dragons and griffins, are depicted as carnivorous predators that prey on other animals or mythical beings. Others, like unicorns, are believed to subsist on a diet of pure water, fresh vegetation, and the essence of flowers. Still, others, such as mermaids and selkies, are associated with the bounty of the sea and may consume fish or other marine life.

Quirky Behaviour: Mystical creatures often exhibit quirky and fantastical behaviours that set them apart from ordinary animals. For example, dragons are known for their love of shiny objects and hoarding treasure, while unicorns are elusive and solitary beings that possess magical healing powers. Some mythical creatures, like the phoenix, undergo cyclical processes of death and rebirth, symbolizing eternal renewal and regeneration. Others, like the kraken or the Loch Ness Monster, are shrouded in mystery and intrigue, with sightings and legends fueling speculation about their existence.

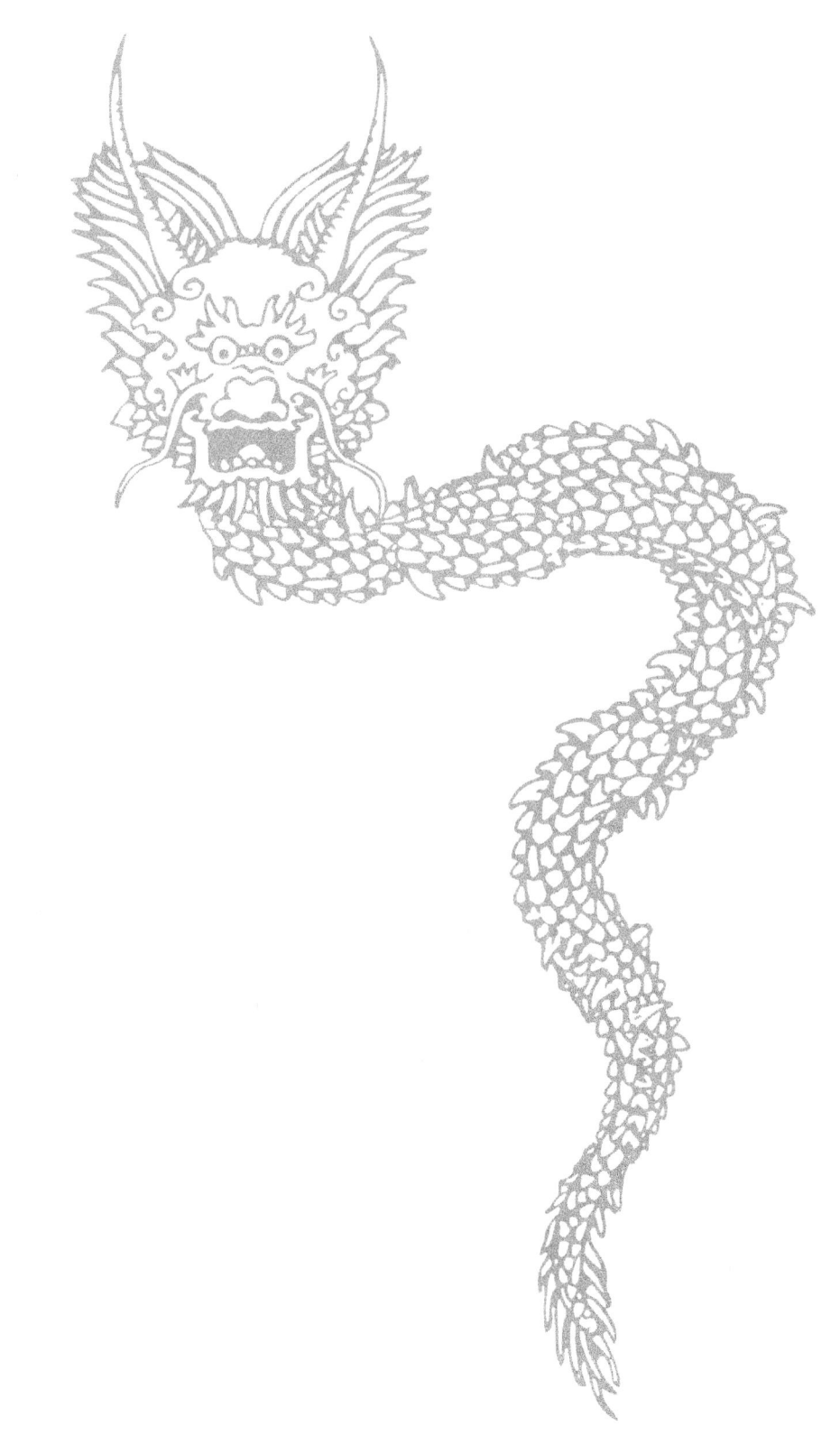

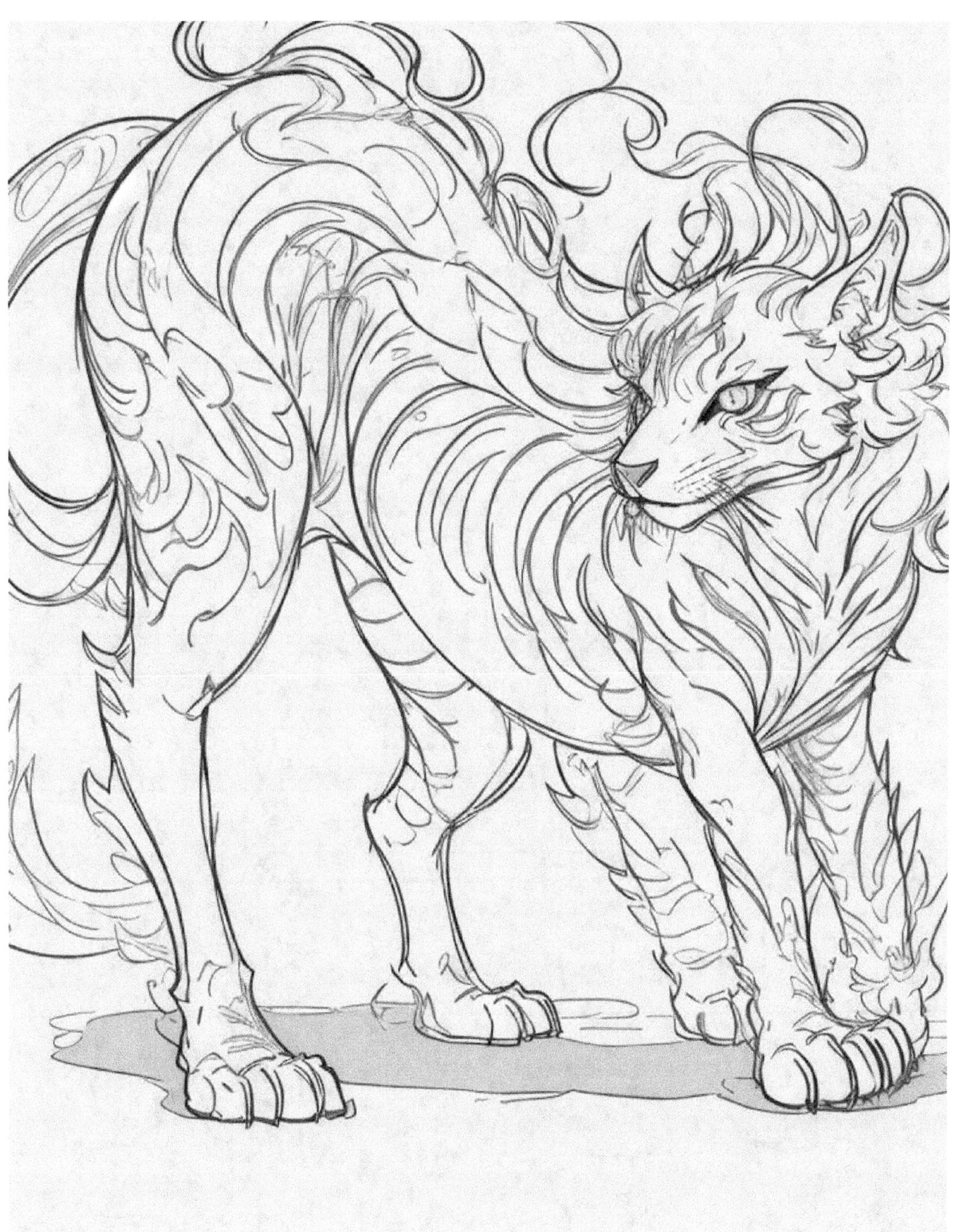

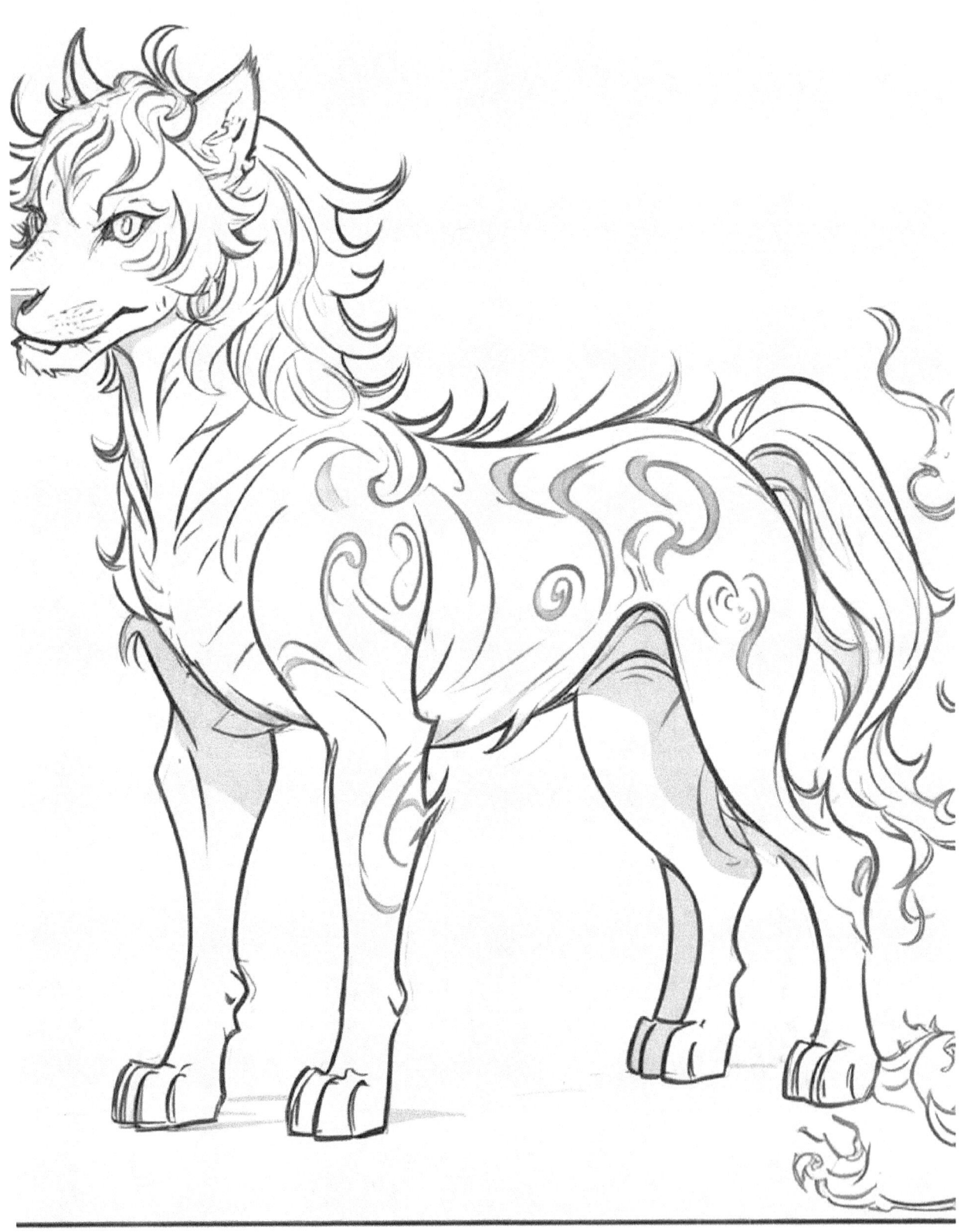

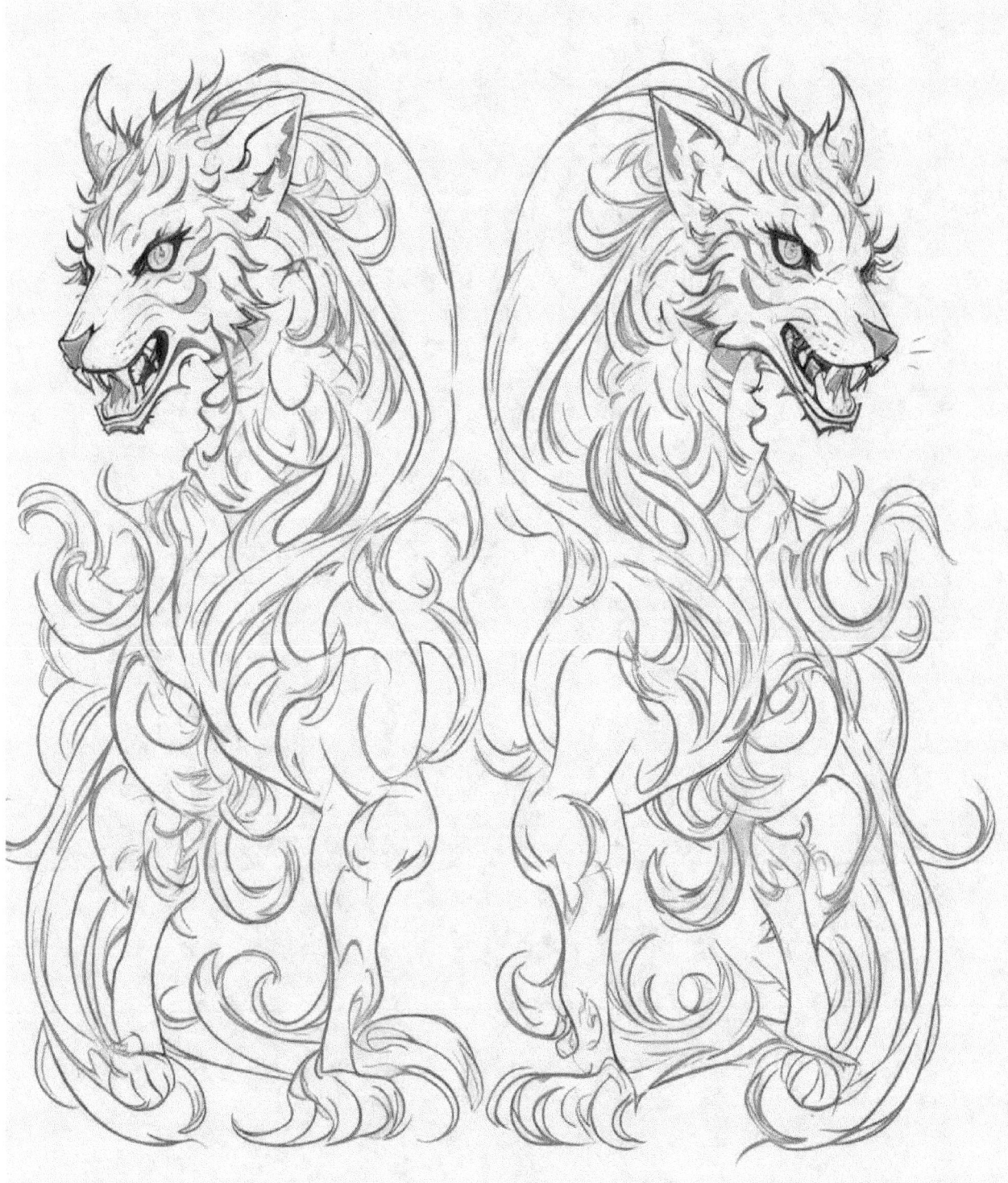

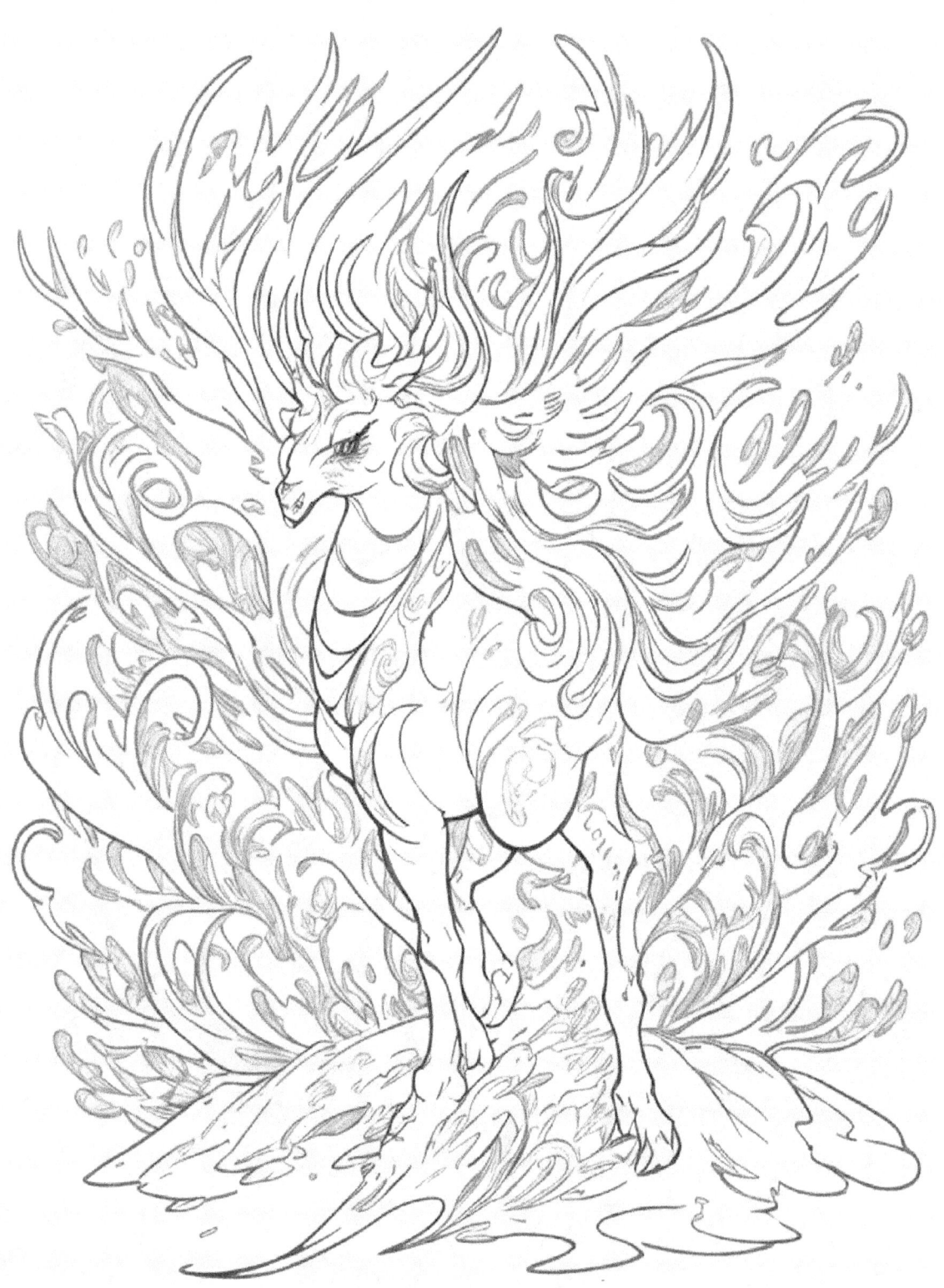

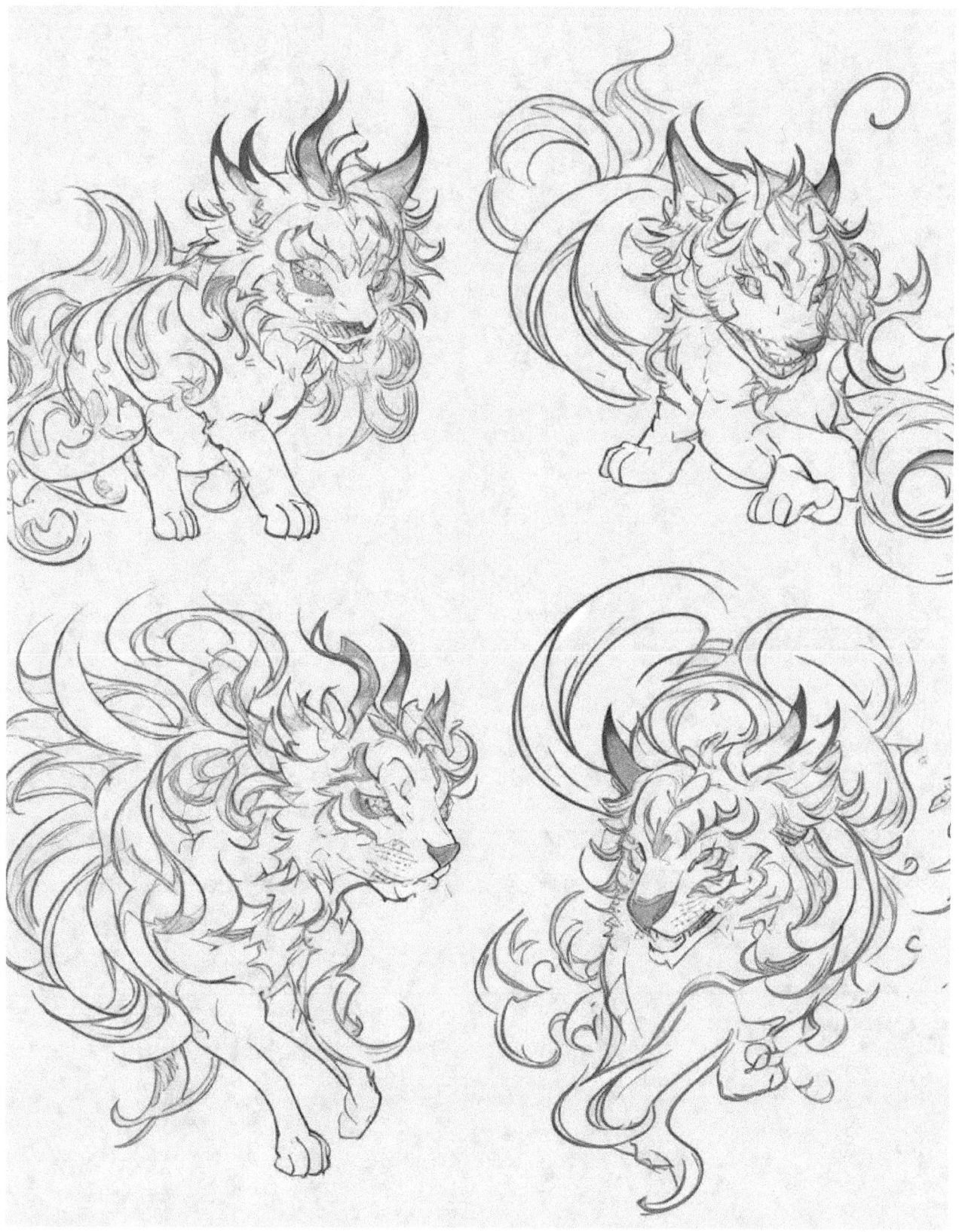

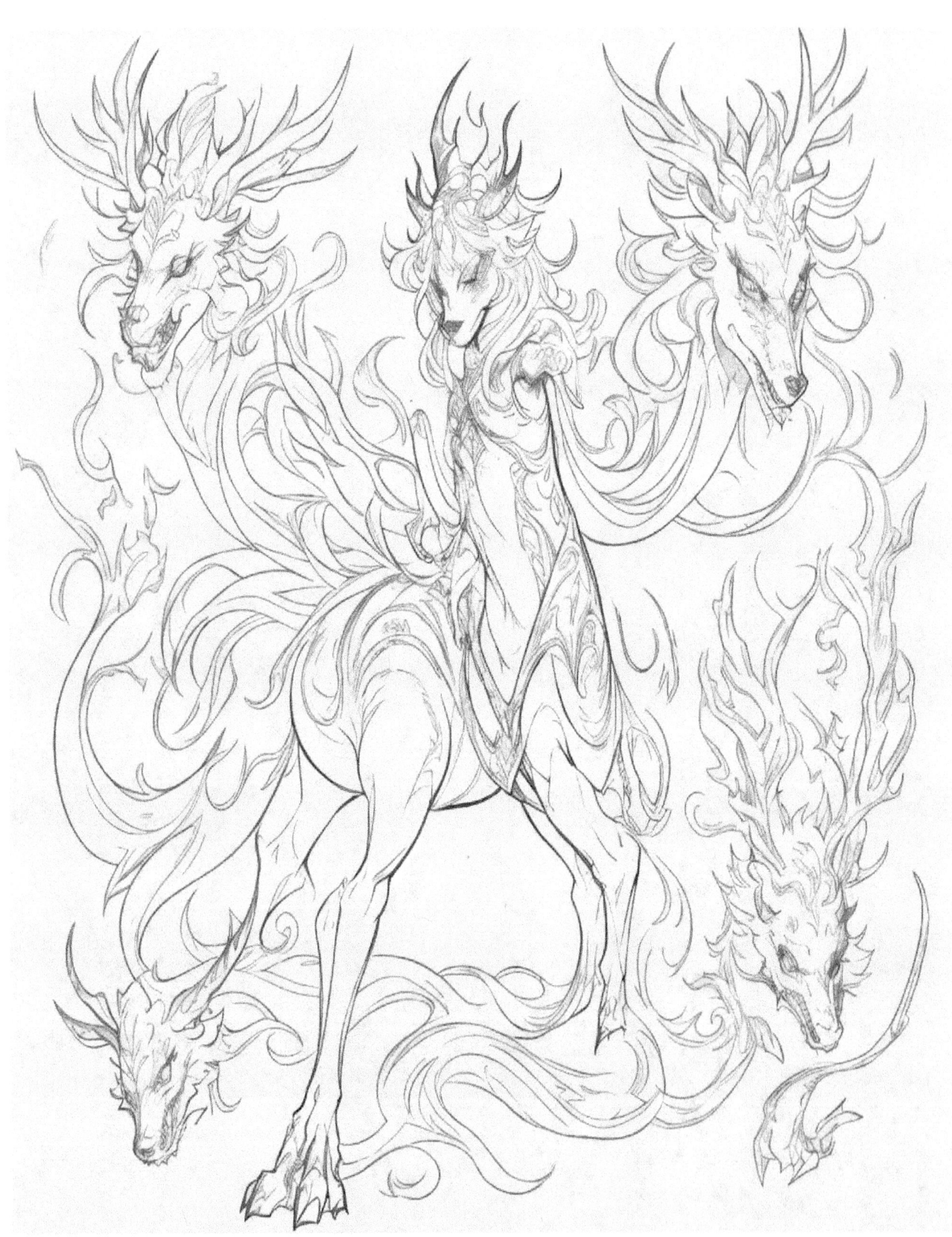

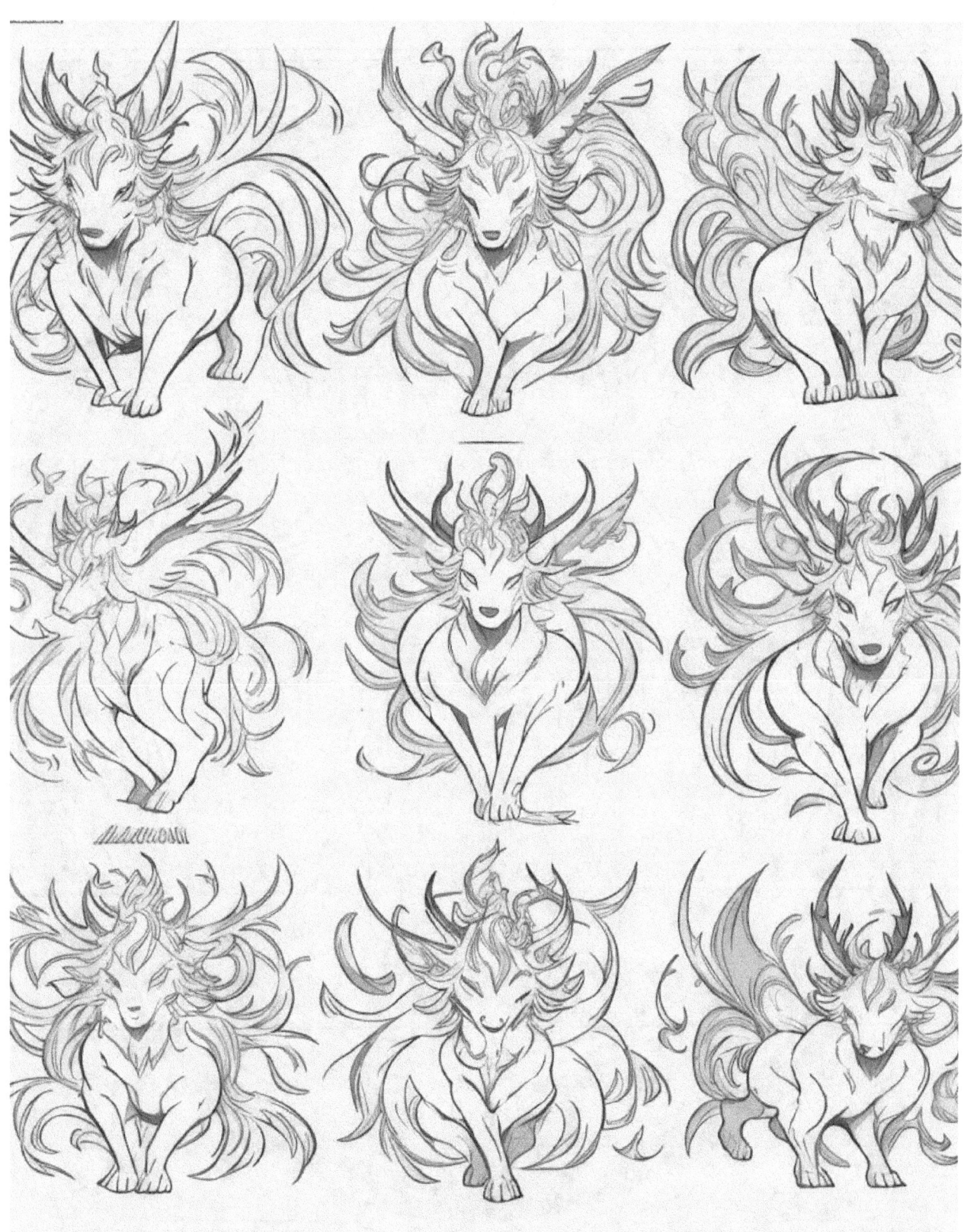

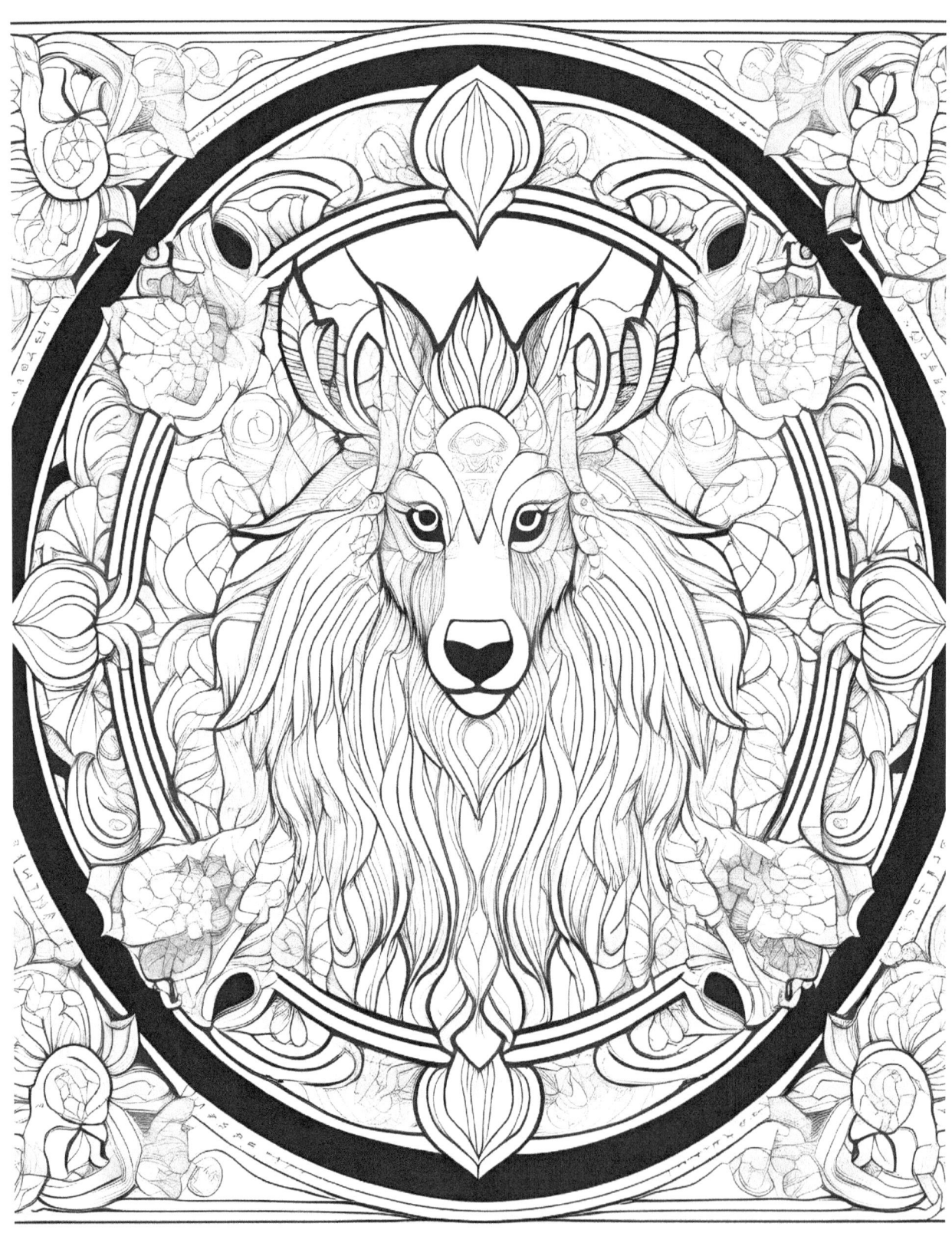

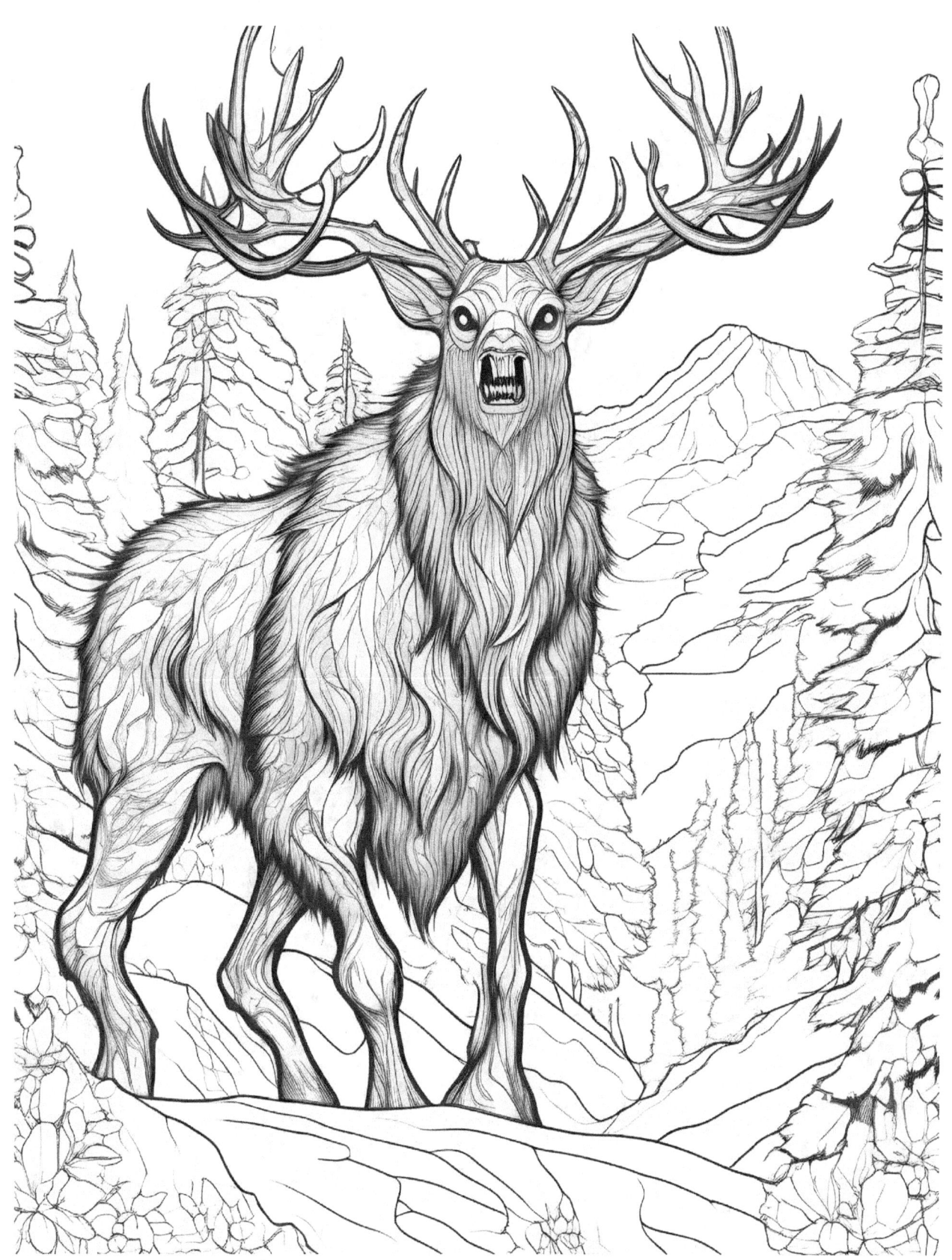

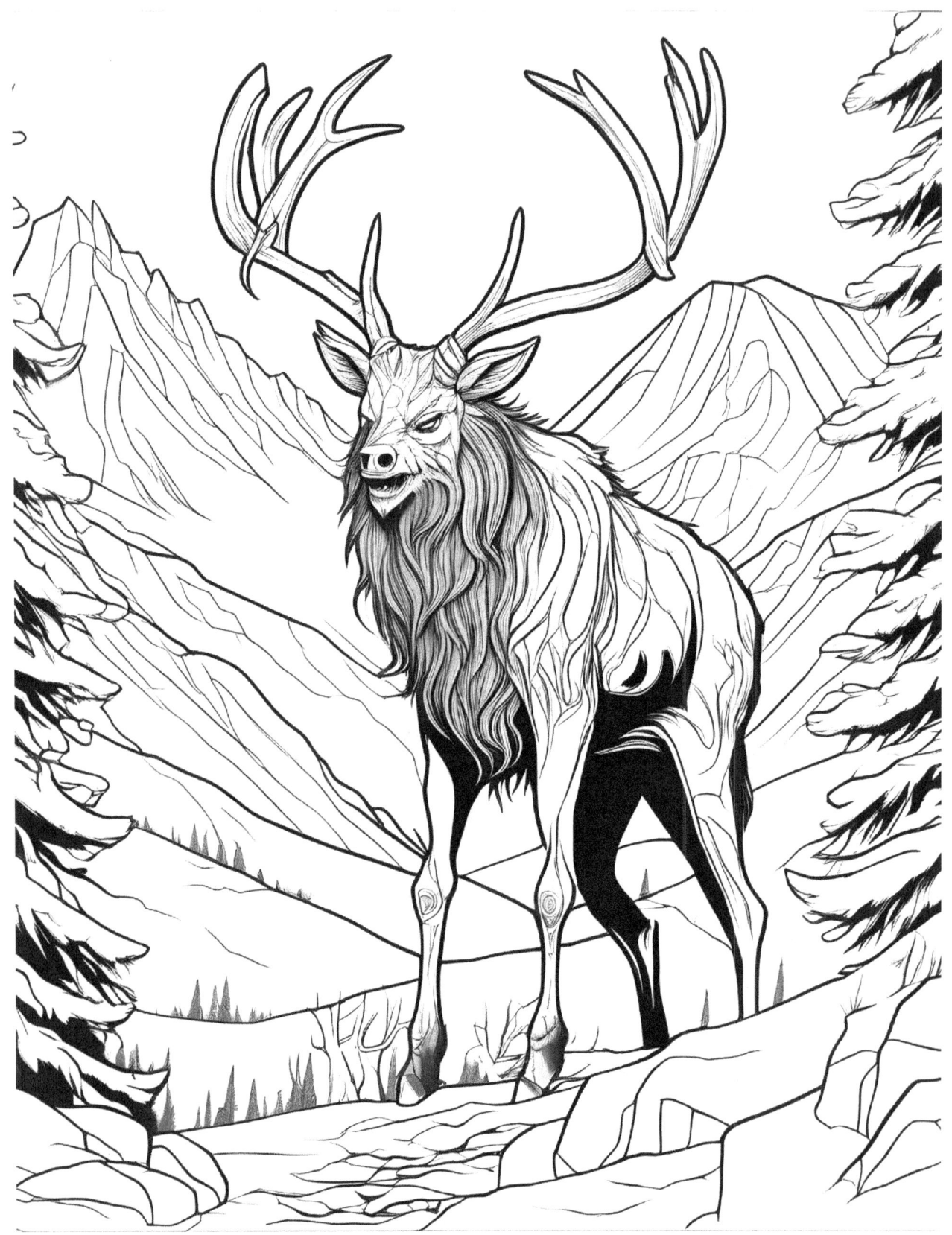

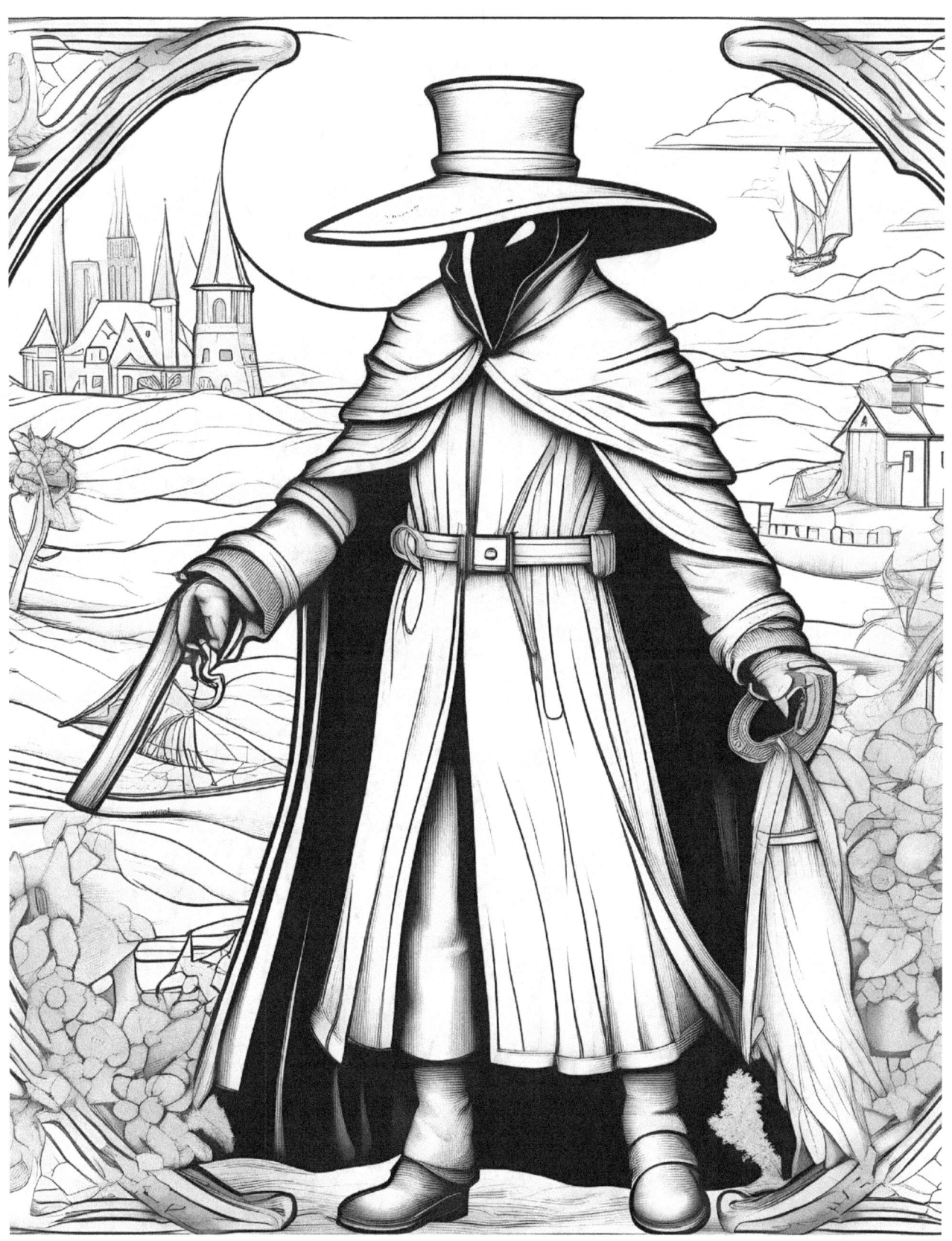

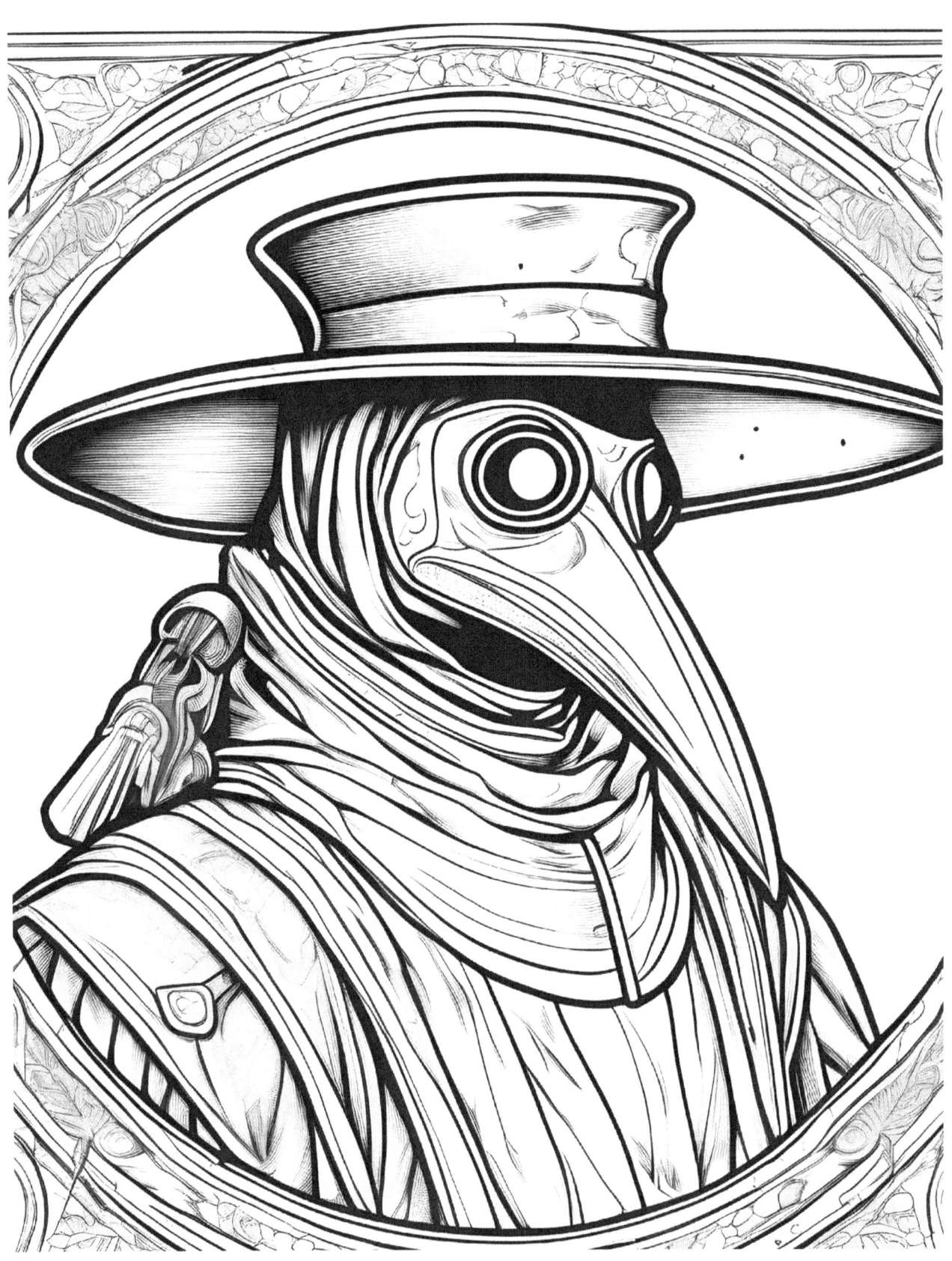

Fairies

Habitat: Fairies are believed to inhabit enchanted forests, shimmering glens, and secluded meadows, where the veil between the mortal realm and the mystical world is thinnest. These magical beings are closely connected to nature, often dwelling in harmony with the flora and fauna of their surroundings. Their habitats are depicted as idyllic and otherworldly, filled with vibrant colours, fragrant flowers, and sparkling streams that reflect their whimsical and ethereal nature.

Food: In folklore, fairies are often depicted as feasting on ethereal delicacies such as nectar, honeydew, and ambrosia, which are said to sustain them and imbue them with magical powers. They are also associated with the harvest and agricultural fertility, bestowing blessings upon crops and sharing in the bounty of the land. Fairies are known for their love of sweets and treats, and offerings of milk, honey, and baked goods are often left out to appease them and seek their favour.

Quirky Behaviour: One quirky behaviour associated with fairies is their mischievous and playful nature. Fairies are known for their love of pranks and tricks, delighting in bewildering and perplexing unsuspecting mortals with their magical antics. They are believed to possess the ability to shape-shift, vanish into thin air, and cast enchantments that bewilder the senses and confound the mind. Fairies may also exhibit capricious behaviour, alternating between acts of benevolence and mischief, depending on their mood and the whims of the natural world.

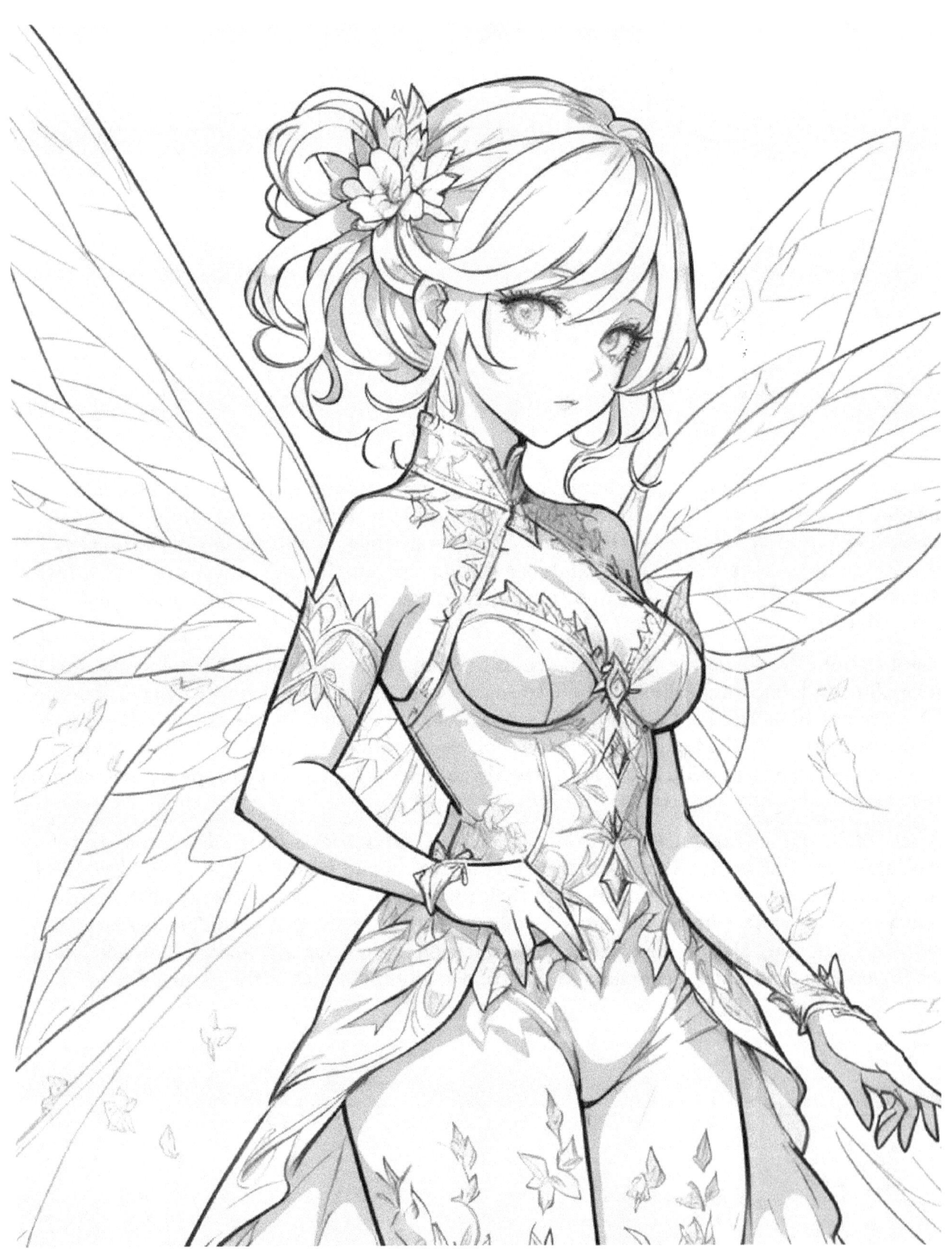

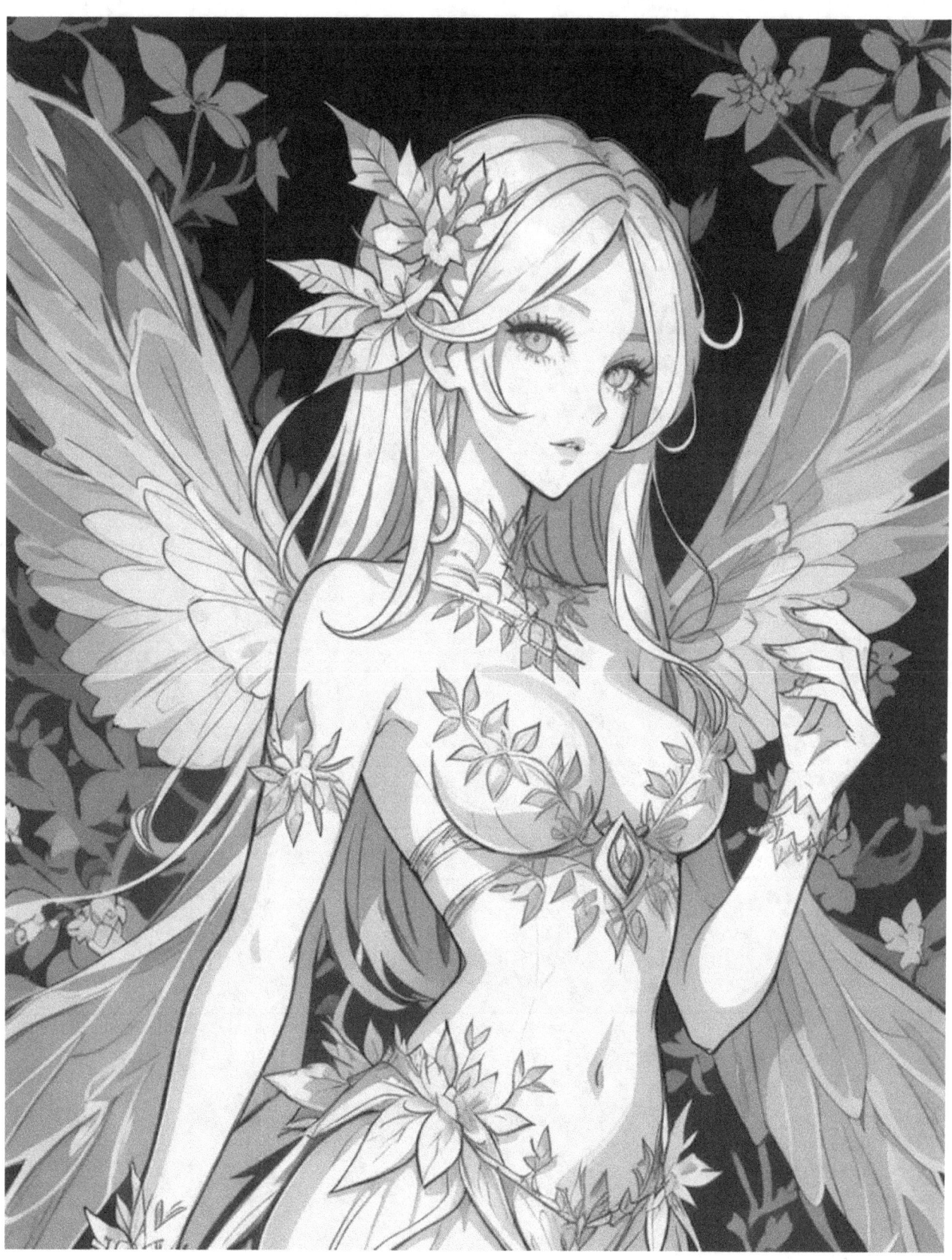

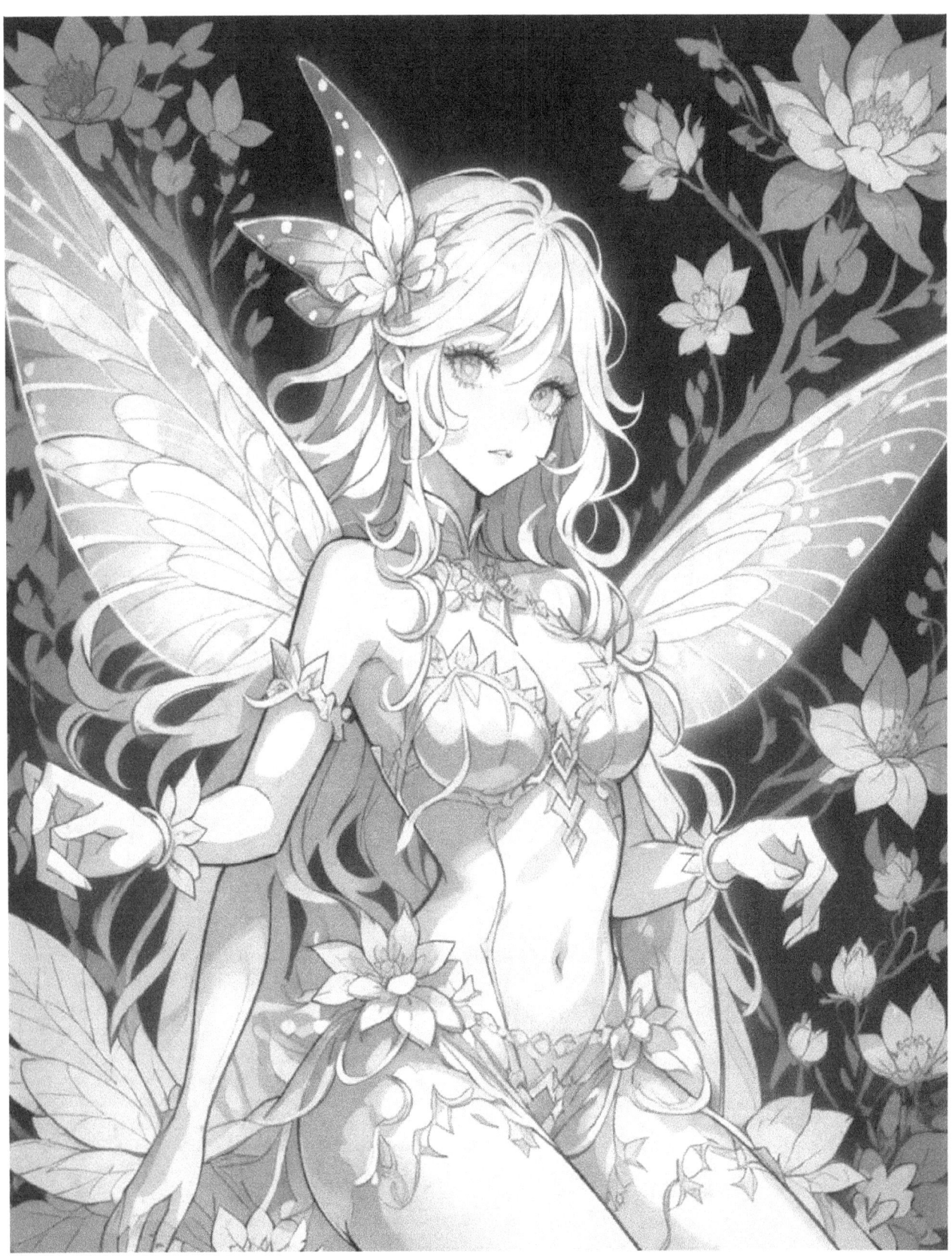

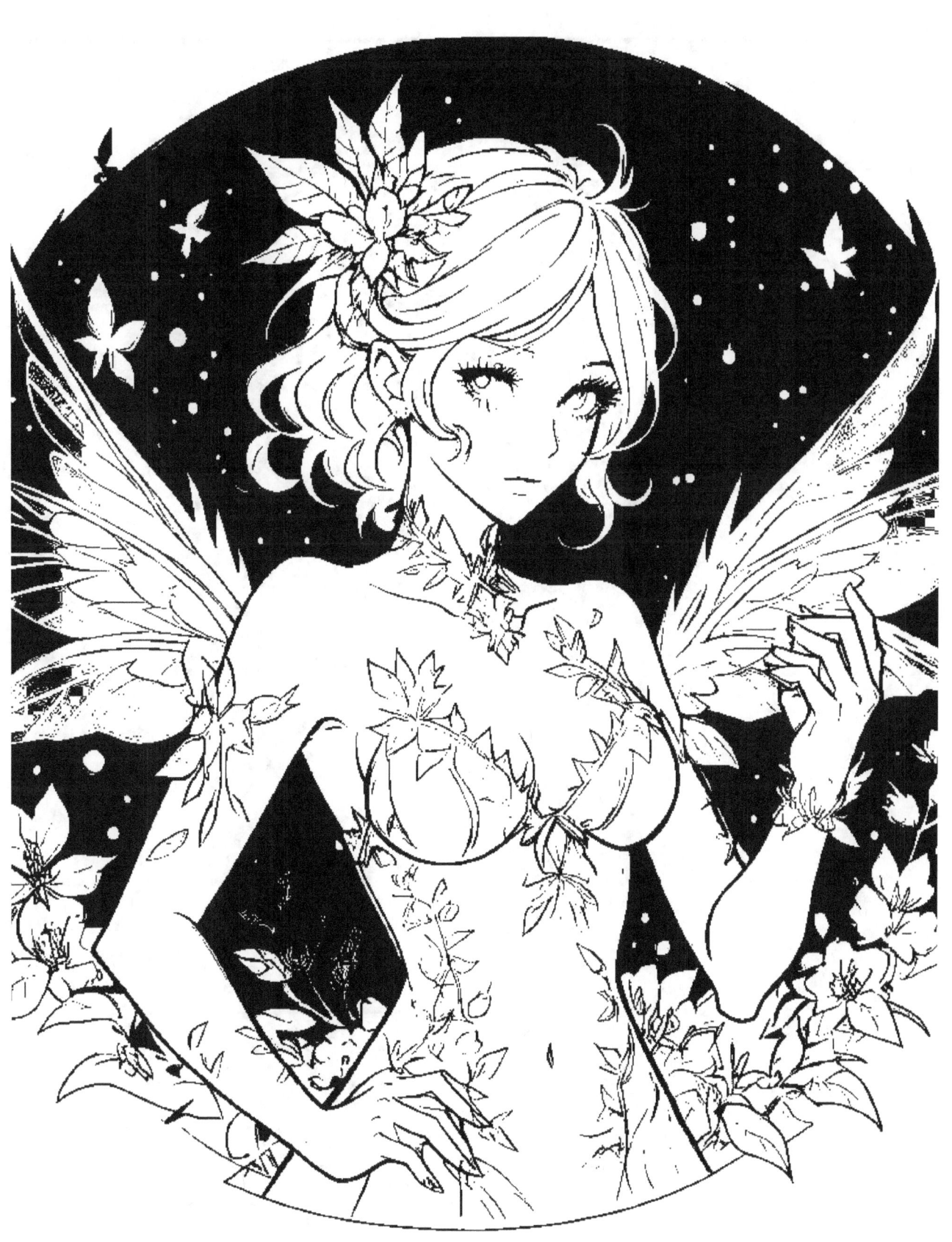

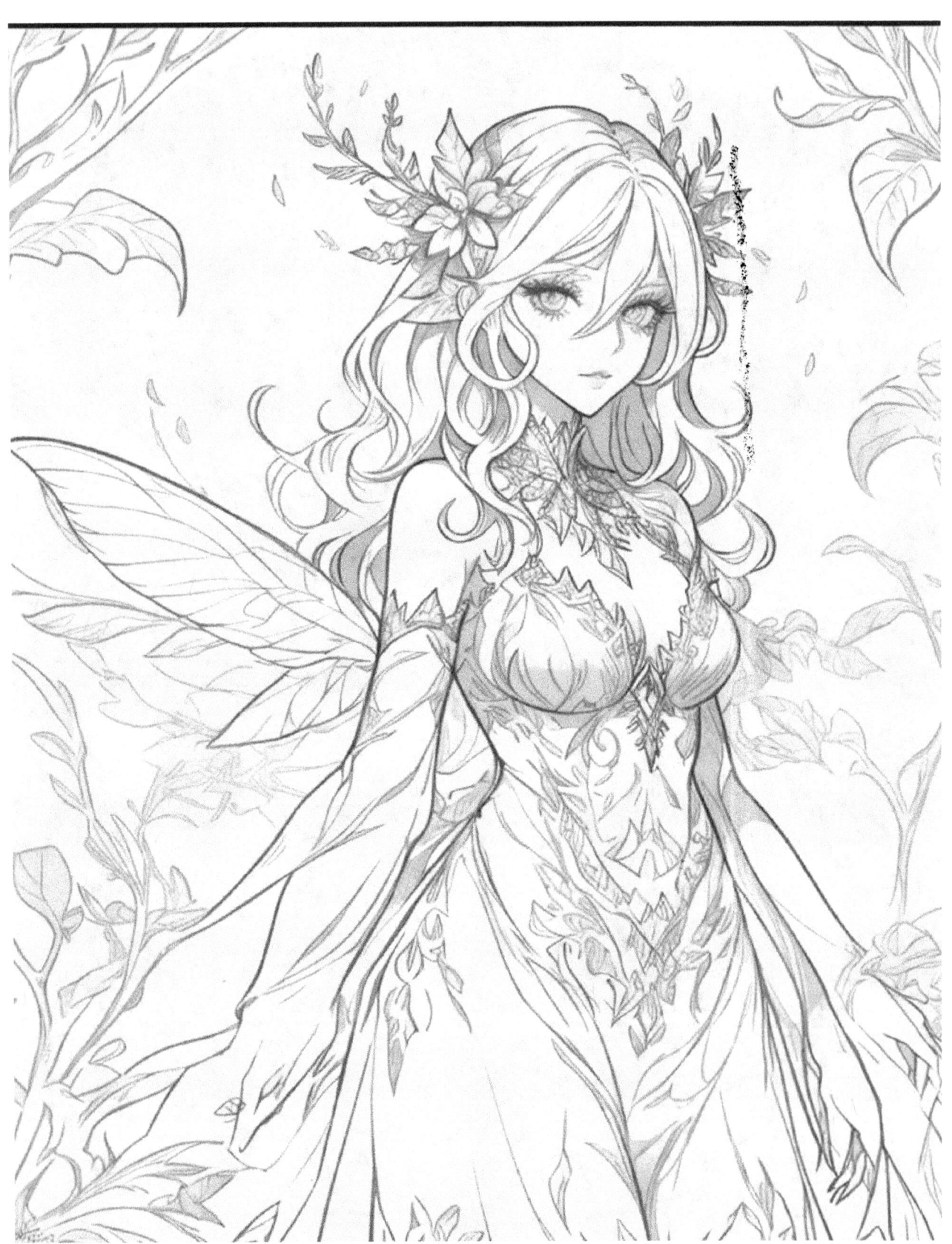

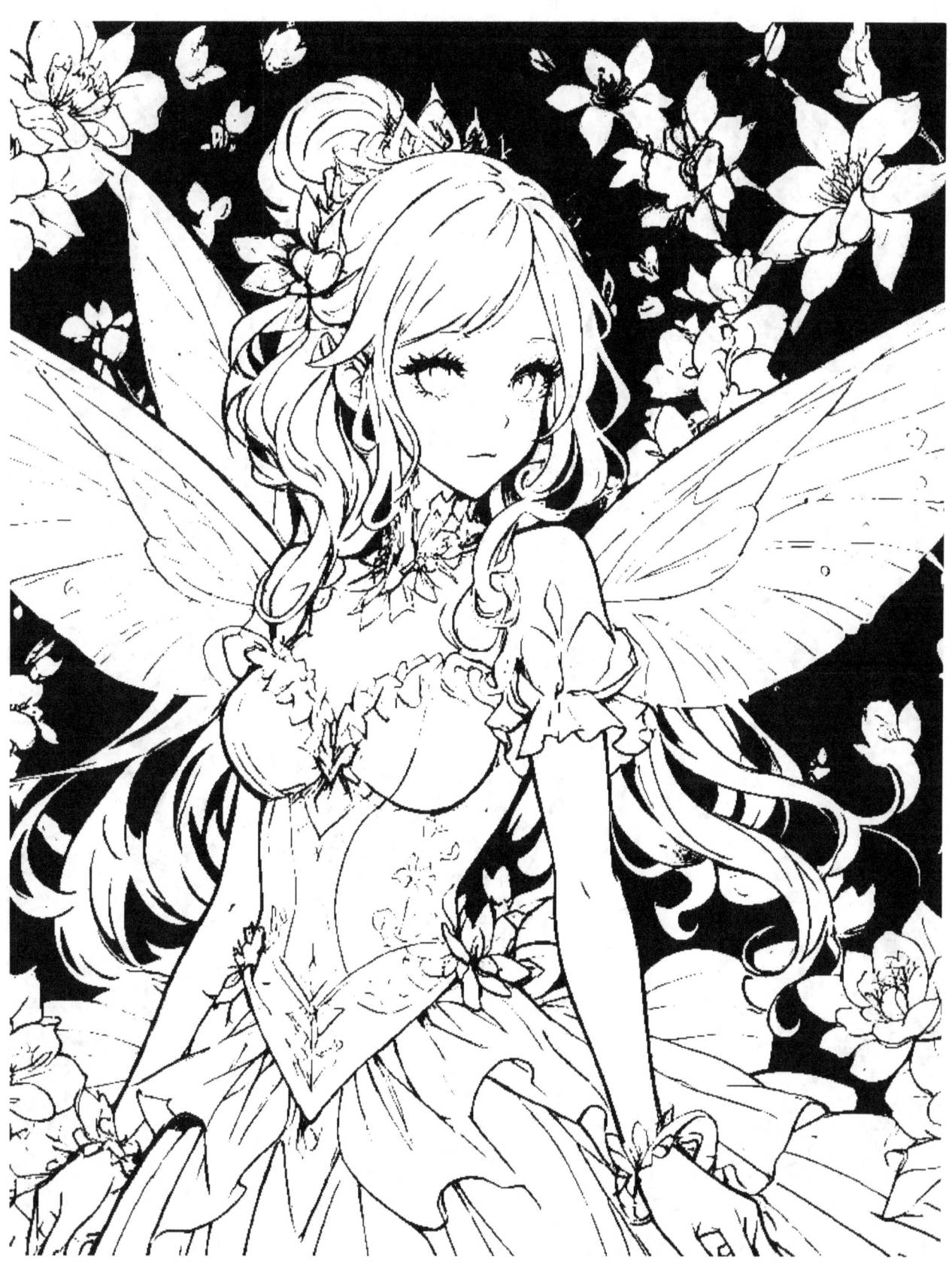

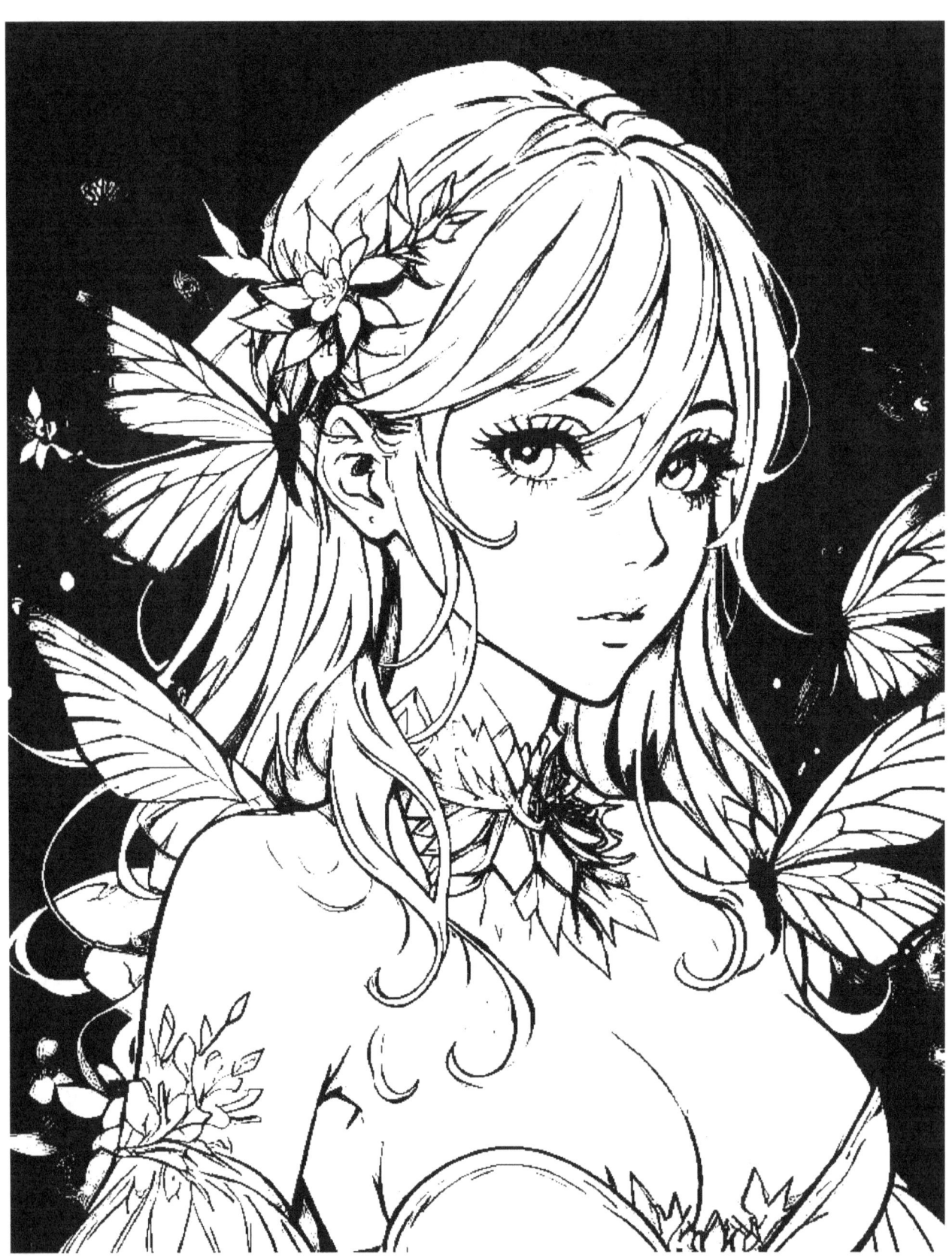

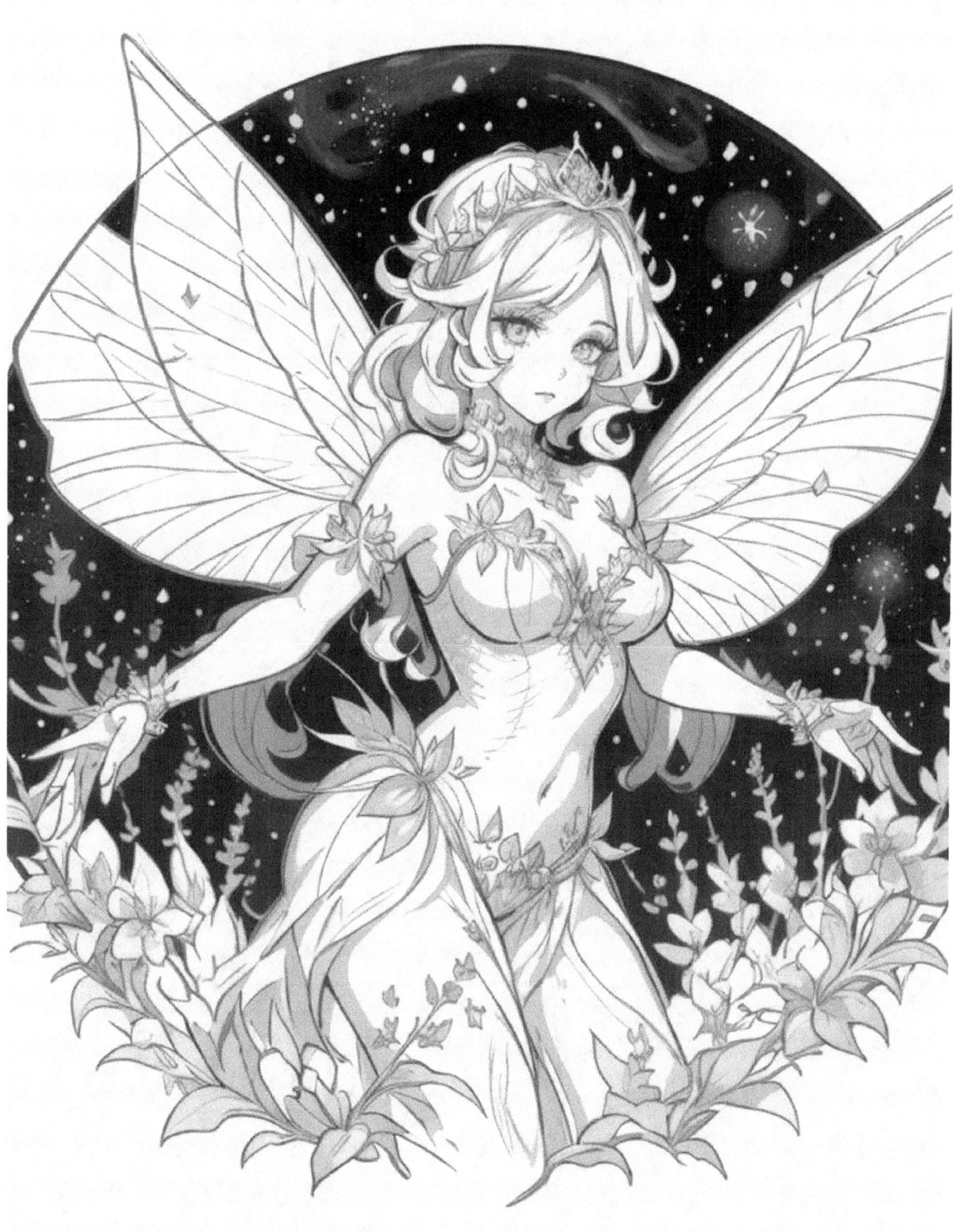

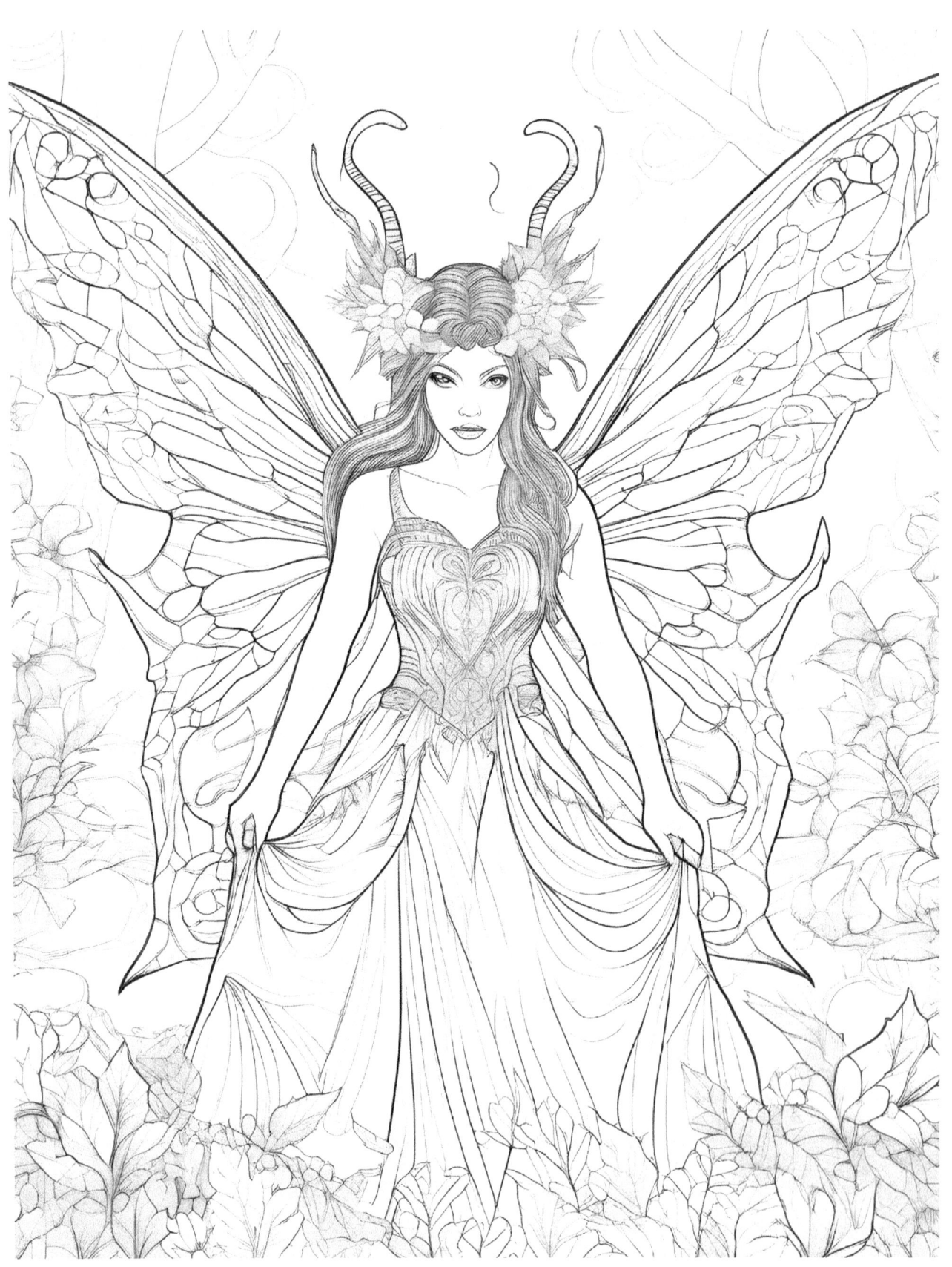

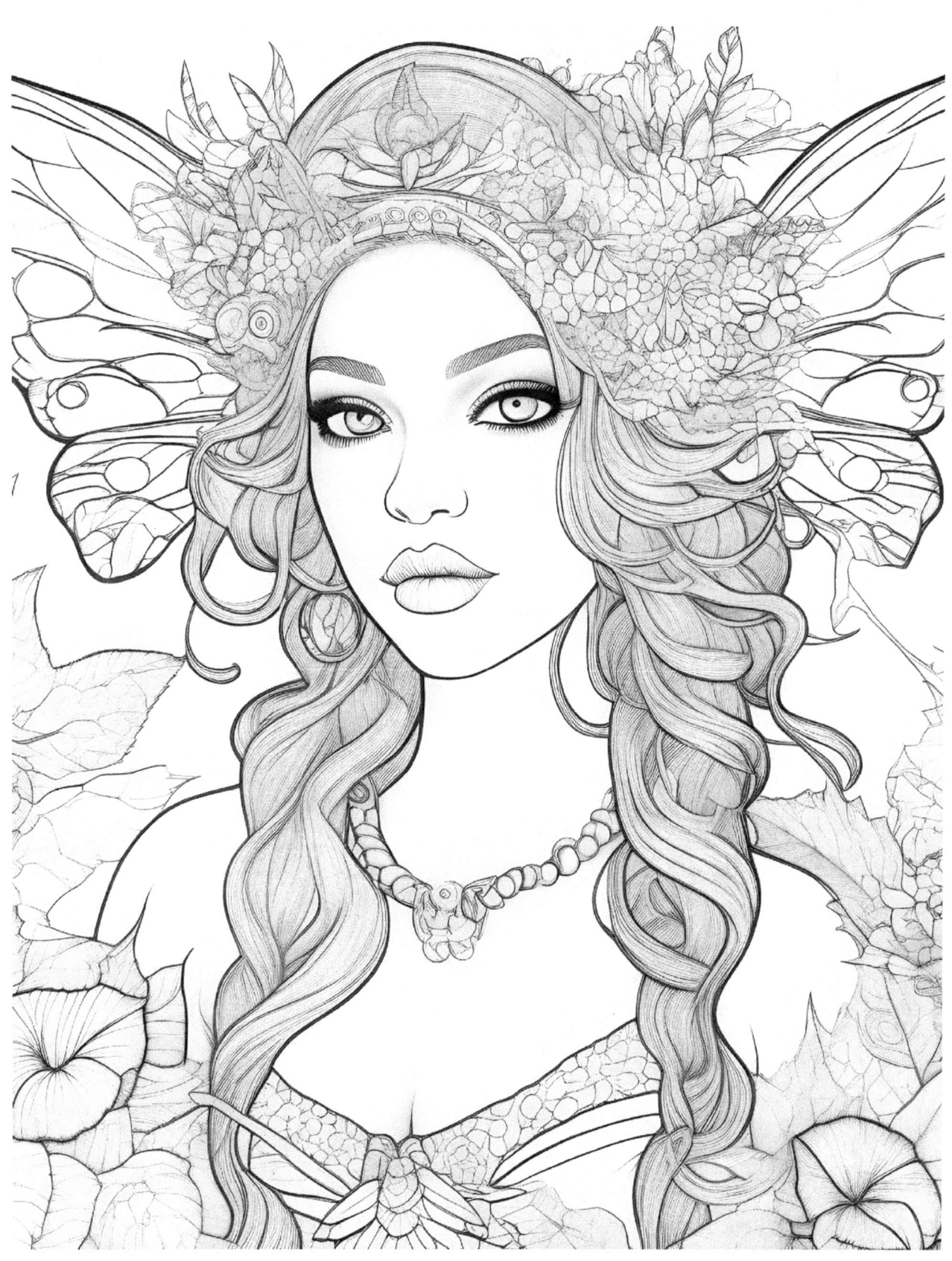

Skulls

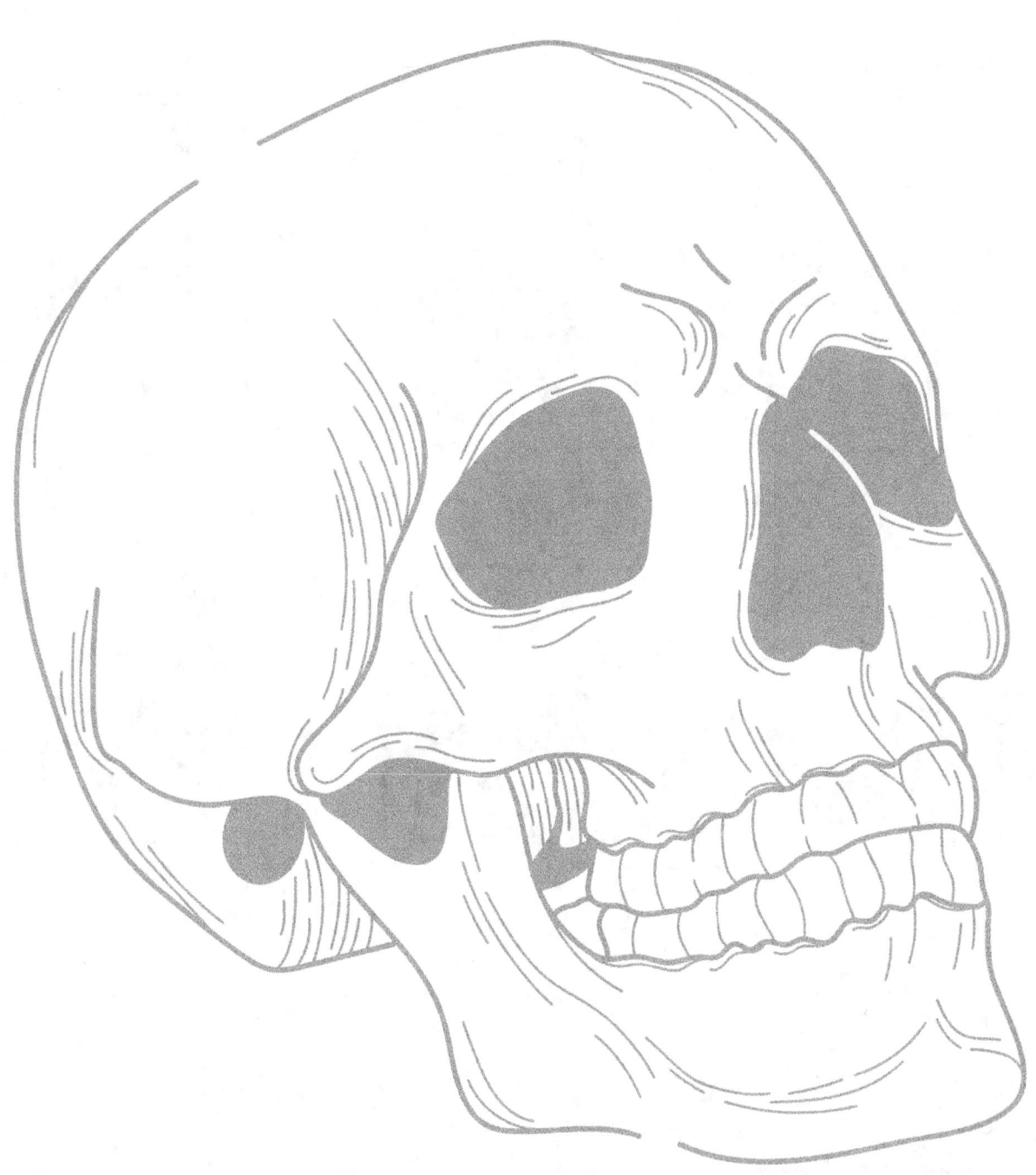

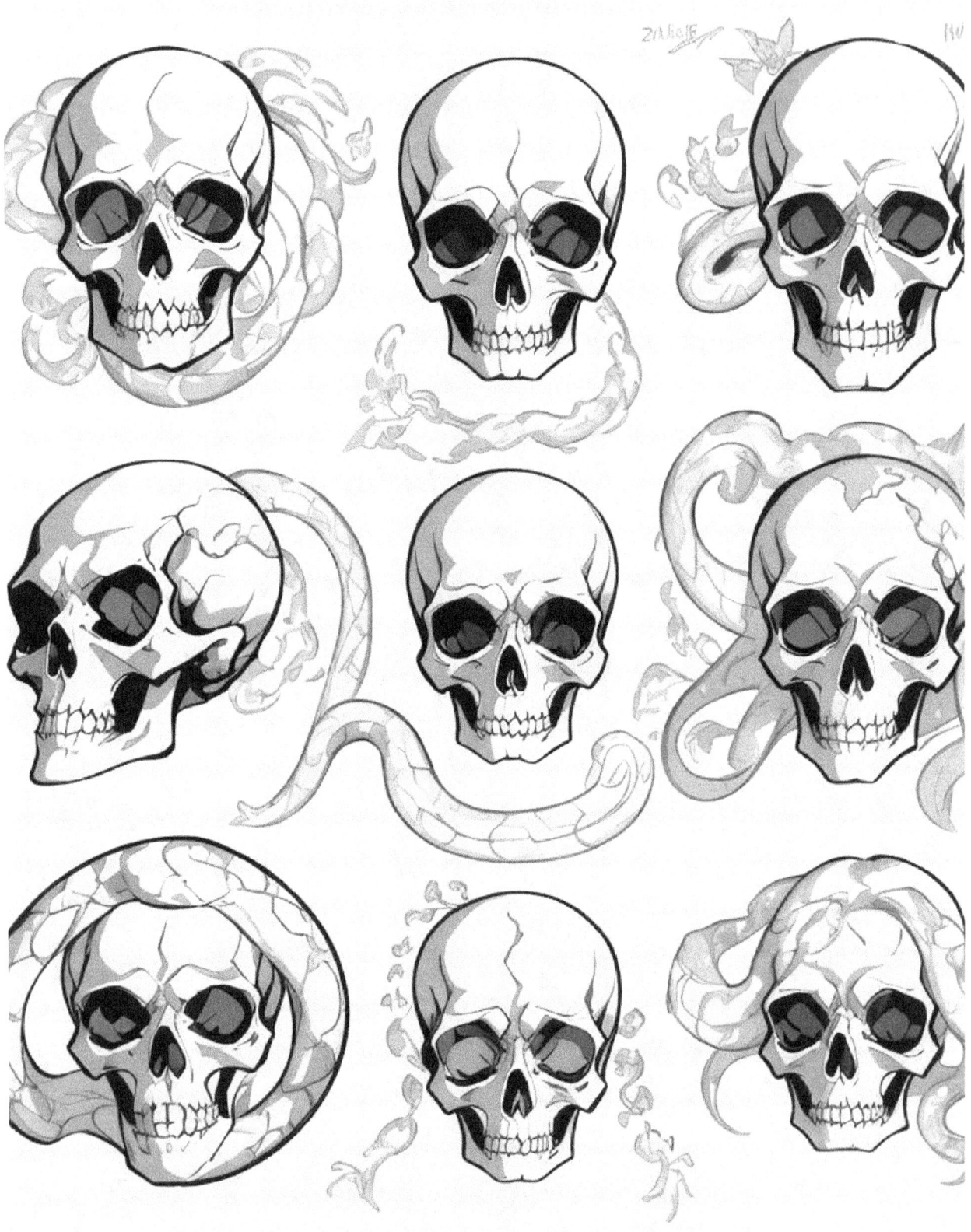

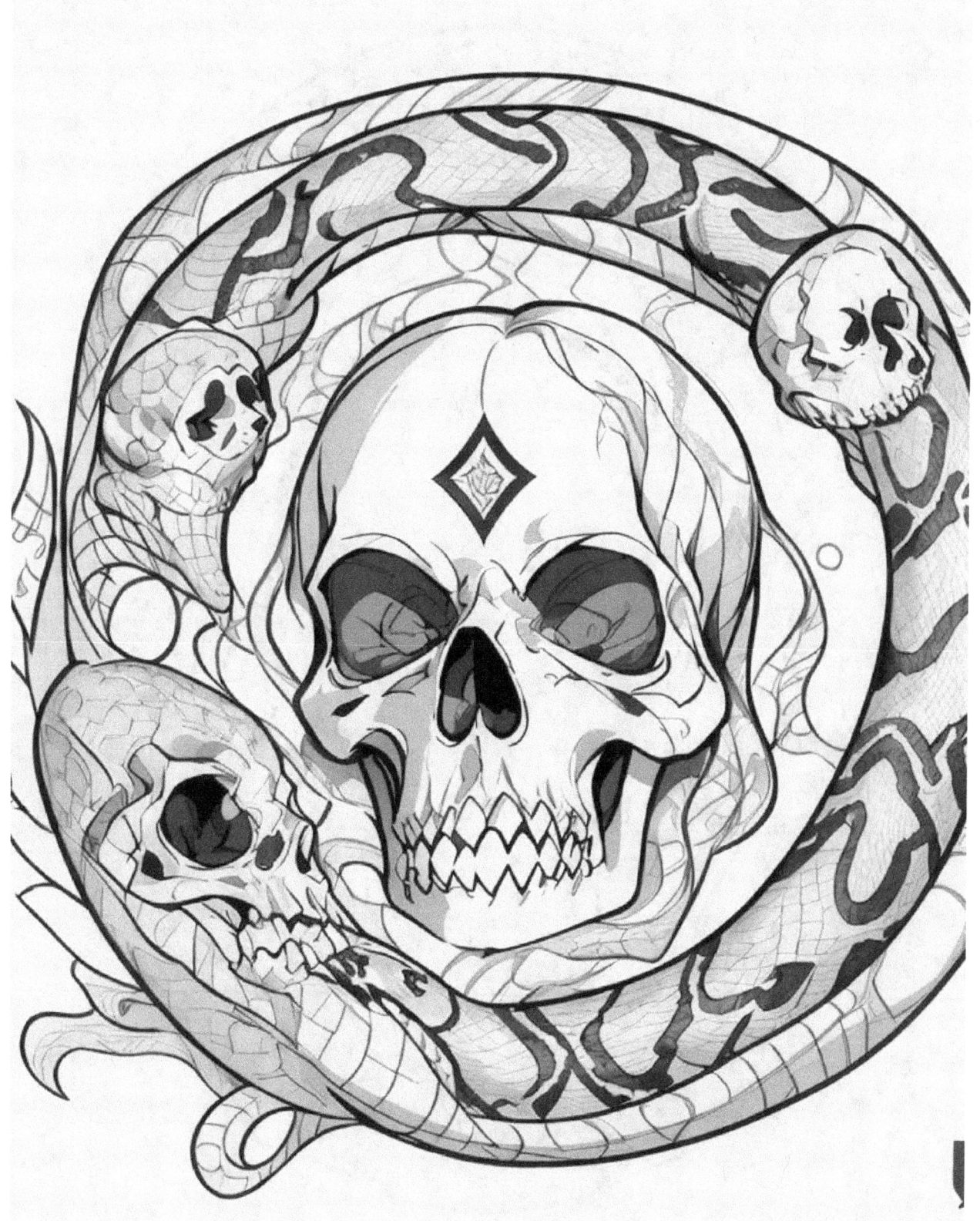

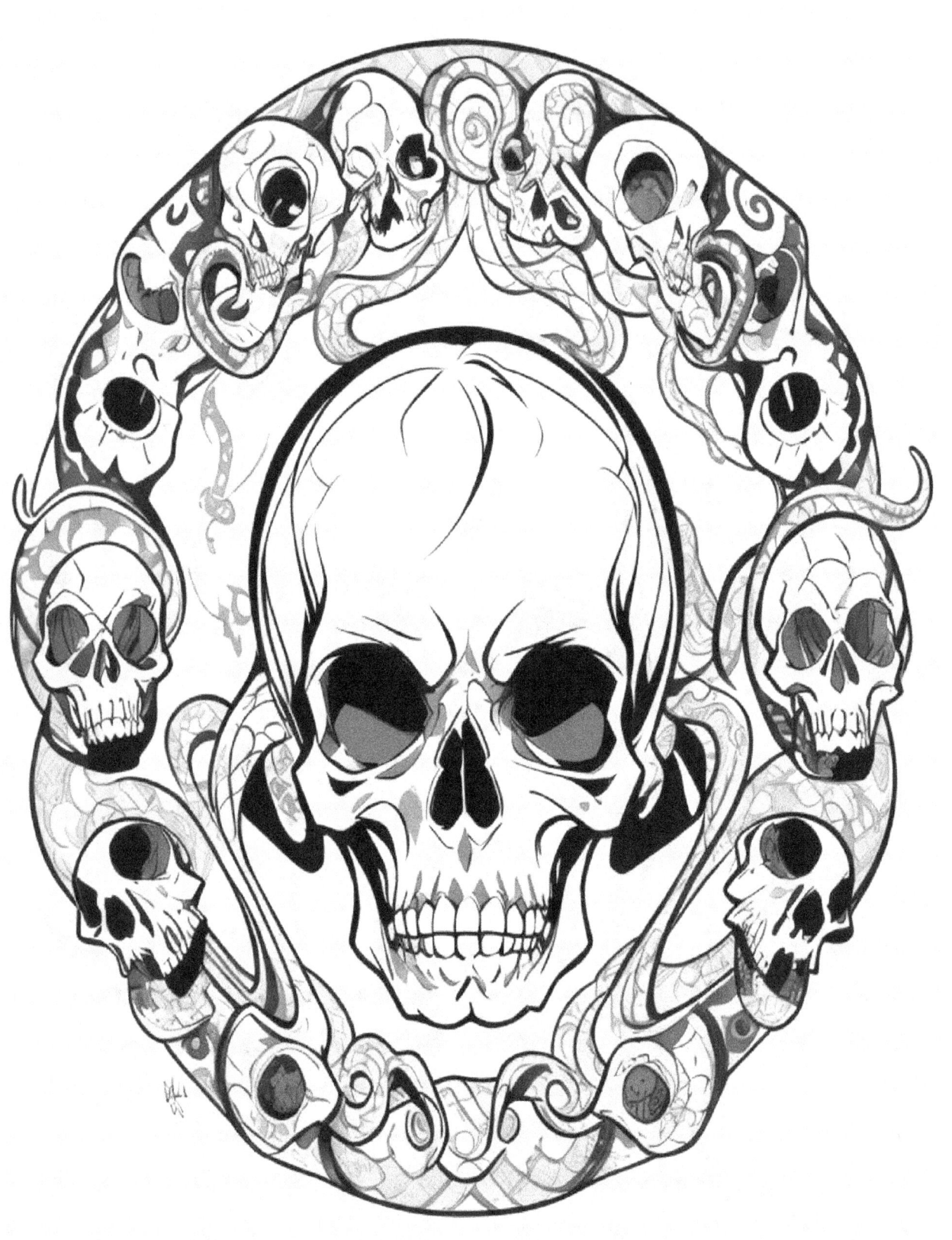

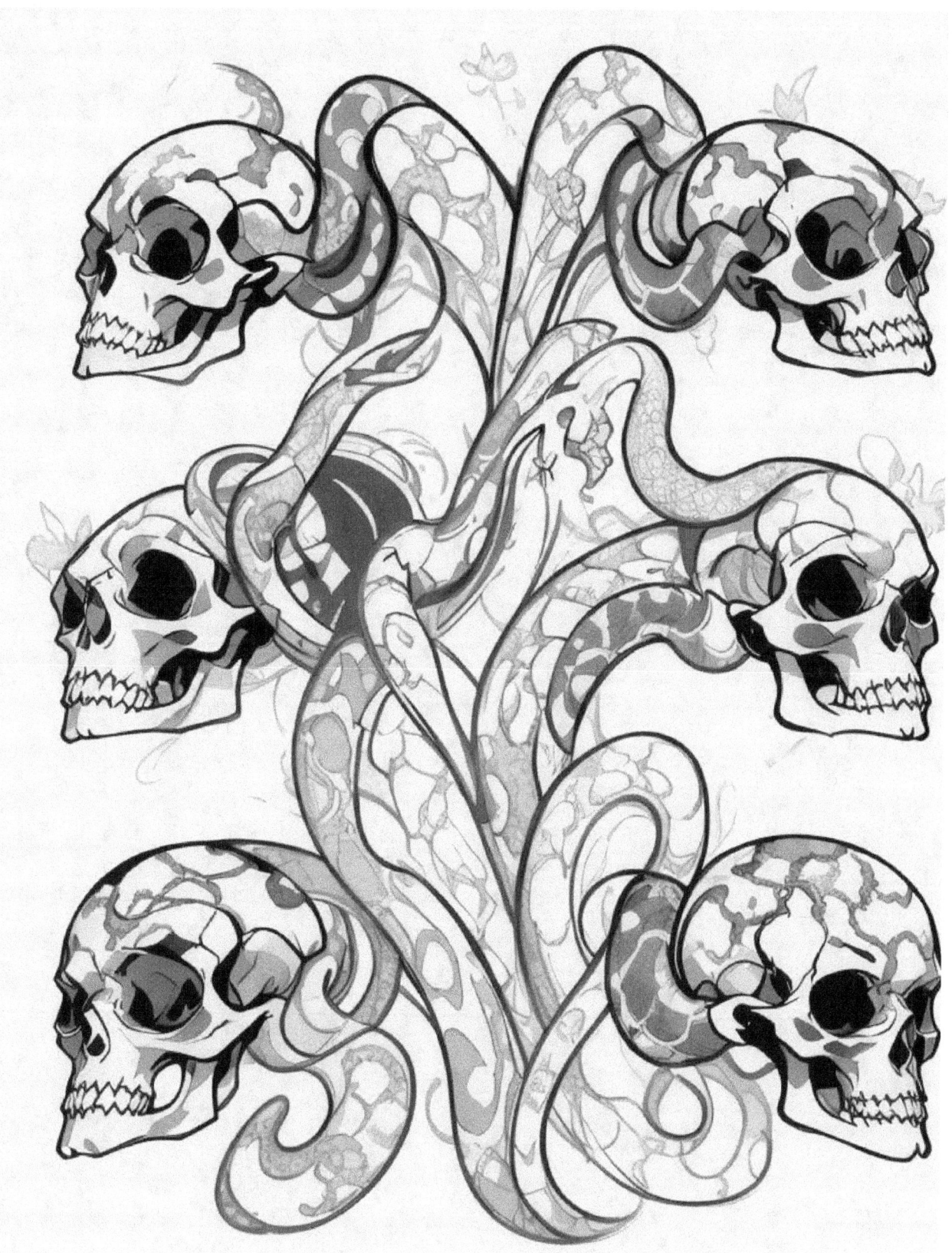